To Marion,
Enjoy the symbolism.

Jacqueline Murray
1991

The Power of Dress

An Insider's Guide to Corporate Dress and Culture

Your clothes
speak
even before
you do.

The Power of Dress

An Insider's Guide to Corporate Dress and Culture

Jacqueline Murray

with

Toni Nebel

Illustrations by Stella Clay

Photography by Liza Fourré

A Semiotics Book · Minneapolis

Photography by Liza Fourré
Illustrations by Stella Clay

First Edition

Library of Congress Cataloguing-in-Publication Data
Murray, Jacqueline
   The power of dress: an insider's guide to corporate dress and culture
   1. Clothing and dress   2. Nonverbal communication (psychology)
   3. Fashion   4. Corporate culture
   I. Nebel, Toni   II. Title

ISBN 0-9625230-0-3

About the Author

Jacqueline Murray, whose background embraces clothing design and psychological counseling, established one of the first image consulting firms in this country over a decade ago. The firm found its niche in two distinct markets: developing of service strategies for retailers and consulting on dress psychology and image for organizations.

Ms. Murray, a consultant for the Dayton Hudson Department Stores, has been instrumental in the development of one of the most successful in-house personal shopping and wardrobe planning services in the U.S. Her seminar, *The Power and Influence of Dress*, has been presented to major corporations and organizations including Honeywell, NSP, NCR, Marquette Banks, Century 21, EDS, IBM, and 3M.

Ms. Murray has also developed and implemented Mode Plus, a personal shopping service for the Galeries Lafayette, one of Paris's major department stores. She lives and works in Minneapolis, Minnesota.

Toni Nebel has written articles, workshops, and scripts. She lives in Minneapolis, Minnesota.

Acknowledgements

I sincerely wish to thank all those who have helped me turn a philosophy I have followed for the last twelve years into *The Power of Dress: An Insider's Guide to Corporate Dress and Culture.*

My heartfelt appreciation to:

Gloria Hogan for her sharp eye and intelligent editing;

Liza Fourré for the wonderful photography which captures the essence of our subjects with sensitivity and insight;

Stella Clay for her exquisite illustrations;

Fred Jackson for his generosity in introducing me to a number of wonderful subjects in this book;

My sister Rosebud who backed my first business venture;

My sister Pat who has always been crazy about me, who protected me all my life, and who thought I would be "great" from day one;

My eternal backers, my children, Guy, Paris, Tiffany, and Caprice (it already sounds like a novel), who taught me that we are living in the present with sometimes obsolete rules and by changing and letting go, I could continue to capture their interest and gain their cooperation;

My wonderful friends who were interviewed and "analyzed" and filled my seminars (sometimes over and over) in my start-up days when I needed bodies;

My enormous family who, through the sheer act of living with them, taught me how to navigate through a corporation;

Those who contributed invaluable time and wisdom, sharing so graciously, openly, and generously: Raffaella Anderson, Martine Bercu, James Binger, Beverly Chalfen, Juanita Costa, Bob Dillon, Rick Dobbis, Fred Gaines, Roxanne Givens, Theresa Holland, Fred Jackson, Bob Kase, Ken Kelly, Mark Lamia, James Lawrence, Cynthia Mayeda, Sue Metzger, Meg Osman, Jean-Paul Penhoat, Julie Pinkwater, Cora Rose, Jan Schonwetter, Fletcher Wright;

Ann DeLong who backed this dream financially, and otherwise;

Lois Crandell for her constant vigilance, putting deadlines on this venture, thus bringing it into reality;

Marge Tilley for tirelessly hustling, prodding, and cheering it on;

Dayton-Hudson Department Stores for their support of the FYI Wardrobing Service, which, in effect, became a laboratory for much of this research. To:

My FYI staff who provided me with valuable insights and practical suggestions;

The FYI managers who understood early on (sometimes before those managing them did) the need to provide what works, not always what was in style. Because of their tenacity, they helped me create a "business-within-a-business" of over 9,000 clients who were and are excellent research "material;"

Karen Bohnhoff who ushered it in;

Jim Stirrat who let me shape it as I saw it;

Steve Watson who has kept a watchful eye over its progress;

Mary Hughes, who is an excellent backer, supporter, and sometimes "peaceful warrior." She sped this project along and made a hard job three times easier. She, in turn, has said I made her job three times harder!

Bill Hammack who became my best listener;

And all the other generous supporters in the Dayton Hudson Stores who helped this business grow.

Contents

Foreword

Like it or not, most people judge us by what they see. In the first few seconds of meeting someone, they have assessed us, made a judgment, positive or negative, that is often hard to change. And in most cases, we only get one chance to make the right impression, whether we're interviewing for a high level position, meeting with a client for the first time, or being introduced to members of the board of directors of our company.

It's the first impression that counts. That's why it's so important to know that everything about us is right, from the hairstyle, dress, or suit we've chosen to the words we say. Dress is language. In fact, dress bears the same relationship to the body that language does to truth. Dress is a necessary sign, a shorthand to who we are, what we think, and where we're going.

And yet, most of us go through our adult life not thinking much about dress because to do so would be narcissistic, too self-focused. But if we recognize the impact our dress and our appearance have on others, what they communicate to others, we would be more careful in selecting what we wear to face the world.

This book is about dress—not fashion, nor style, although they are certainly a part of all dress. It is about the art of choosing clothes that are eminently appropriate for who we are, what we do, and where we do it. In essence, it is designed to take the mystery out of being well-dressed by teaching you to decipher a suitable dress code.

This is not a book about rules, or promises. This is a book about decoding the business dress process. It will help you to see with your own eyes and through your own experiences how most effectively to operate in the business world. In this book, you will gain an understanding of how dress influences your impact on others. It will help you understand how important your organization's dress culture is in your overall professional life. Hopefully, you can and will use this information to increase your effectiveness in your organization as you learn how to build an appropriate wardrobe and individualize your own style.

The power is yours. Modify your wardrobe, or change it completely, and watch things change in your life—for the better!

1

In the Beginning . . .

"You never get a second chance to make a first impression."
Will Rogers, sage

Kings and queens know it's important. So does the military. So do countless organizations with images to preserve.

What is IT? And why is IT important?

It is *dress*—the total physical impact you make when you appear in public.

It is the *first thing* an observer sees.

It is the *critical factor* in how others judge you, accept or reject you.

It is the series of *messages* and *symbols* you send out daily about yourself.

And for most of us, IT is a largely unconscious message, often not what we intended at all. Pretty powerful, that IT!

How does that happen, you ask? It happens because most of us only recognize at some subconscious level that the clothes we choose have symbolic significance. We're all familiar with other kinds of symbols—symbols like the flag, a plain gold band, a brass ring—and what they mean. So too, the clothes we wear send specific messages. Our clothes, like a shorthand system, signal to others whether we're frivolous or serious, cheerful or sad, powerful or powerless, friend or foe, a team player or a loner.

The Power of Dress

Clothing is a wonderful doorway that most easily leads you to the heart of an individual; it's the way they reveal themselves.
— Tom Wolfe, quoted in *TIME*

Like it or not, most people judge us by what they see. In the first few seconds of meeting, he or she has subconsciously made a judgment about us—positive or negative—that is hard to change. Whether we're interviewing for a high level position, meeting with a client for the first time, or being introduced to members of the board of directors of our company, or asking for a date, we get only one chance to make the right impression.

Dress, especially business dress, is more than our public skin. It is comprised of a series of messages and symbols that are "just as apt to betray and mislead us as they are to express and convey—with or without intent," according to Alison Lurie, in *The Language of Clothing.* She says that Balzac, in *Daughter of Eve,* observed that dress is "a continual manifestation of intimate thoughts, a language, a symbol." Today, semeiologists and sociologists reiterate the notion that dress is a language of signs, a nonverbal system of communication.

All of us know this, mostly on a subconscious level. We meet people on the street, in corporations, in the living of life, and intuitively, instinctively, we know things about them: their occupation, their birthplace, personality, opinions, tastes, moods. We may not be able to put what we observe into words, but we register the information subconsciously and make judgments accordingly. Or, more accurately, we have immediate conditioned responses shaped by cultural imperatives.

Clothing is packaging. The fig leaf was the first fashion creation. Since then, we have come a long way, but the psychology of fashion has changed very little.
— *The Psychology of Fashion*

Right now, you're probably thinking, I know all this. What am I getting? Another book on dress? Haven't we read enough about this? Doesn't everyone know how important dress is? Of course they do. The self-help sections of major booksellers are chock-full of books on dressing for success. More people than ever believe it's important to dress properly for certain occasions. They are aware that appearance is a key factor in creating the right impression. But this concern, this resurgence of interest in how we look, is more than an interest in fashion and being stylish.

Hardly anyone is uninterested in dress. Whether we like to think of ourselves above it all or too individualistic to care what others think, we do form opinions about others, especially of those who dress outside the "norms" of our present experience.

To give you some sense of the power of this subconscious, intuitive, instantaneous reaction, I'd like you to look at the photographs here and on the following pages. Glance at them quickly, as if you were seeing them on television, on a billboard, in a store window, on the street in your city. What kind of feelings do they evoke? What do they symbolize? Do you identify with some more than others?

Photos reprinted with permission of Wide World Photos

Photos reprinted with permission of Wide World Photos

The photographs on the previous pages depict some of the symbols in our world. Did some of them cause sadness? Anger? Hostility? Relief? Did you feel nothing? Did you identify more with some than with others?

Instant Impressions

Instant impressions are formed from a name, a smile, a handshake, and other cues. And like some of the universal symbols you just looked at, the effect clothing has on interactions is as old as dress and adornment. How do we "learn" these reactions? We live in a symbolic environment where virtually all the symbols we learn are acquired through others—our family, the country we're born in, the friends we make as we mature, the company we work for, and the work we do. Clothing defines and describes us to the world. That's probably why you found yourself reacting strongly to the photographs of Marilyn Monroe, the Nazi swastika, or the punk youth.

It's important, then, to understand this language and to make it work for us in the same way that we learn to speak a language. We want to communicate effectively and consciously with those around us, to let others know our status, how powerful we are, where we live, who we are affiliated with, and whether or not we belong (even to what "in" group we belong).

What made you react—favorably or unfavorably—to the pictures on the previous pages? Before you could do anything about it, you had formed a judgment. That's the way it is for all of us. Our reactions are formed by who we are, where we come from, our family system, and our values. They are conditioned responses. They are automatic. They make up who we are. Because these symbols are so much a part of us, it's important that we understand them and that we learn to understand what they say about us and the people with whom we interact.

For example, how did you know that some of the individuals were not Americans? And, conversely, how do non-Americans know that an American is an American? Well, that's easy, you say. Yes, easy to say, but much harder to define. They (or conversely we) just look different. That's all! Whether we're American, French, Italian, Russian, or Lithuanian, we do look different. We carry ourselves differently. We use space differently. Above all, we wear clothes differently. These non-verbal symbols and the way they are used differentiate nationalities and nations.

If you're an American reading this book, picture in your mind's eye what you look like to someone from another country. What distinguishes you from him or her and vice versa? What are the symbols or characteristics that make you most definitely American? If you're a nationality other than American, mentally picture how *you* look to an American. What distinguishes you from him or her? If you're an American male, you might see a well-dressed, smartly put together individual, impeccably groomed, hair coiffed just so, a traditional dark blue pinstripe suit, white shirt, conservative tie. If you're from the West—Denver, Dallas, or Houston—perhaps you're wearing a Stetson and well-crafted boots. If you're from California, you're probably dressed in a lightweight, light-colored Euro-cut suit, a pink or lavender shirt, and bold tie. Your hair is probably a little longer than your East Coast counterpart.

John Jay, senior vice president and creative director for Bloomingdale's, in an article in *GQ*, for example, feels American males "need to show a little more confidence, [look] a little less packaged. . . . a little more adventurous." Of the way Italian men look, Jay says, "You see them on their BMW bikes . . . and all the wrinkles in their suits are wonderful. . . . Most American men would feel that a wrinkled suit just doesn't look presentable."

If you're a French woman, you favor a subtle mix of pattern, shape, and accessories in a near match or unexpected combination of colors.

But if you're an English male, you opt for neat, well-tailored quality clothes with a depth of color or pattern, accented by a boldly striped shirt and patterned tie.

If you look a little closer, you will also notice that even among Americans, or the French, or Italians, there is a "look within a look." For example, there are possibly three to four categories of "look" within each major city of the world, other less well-known cities, and even in the smallest of towns.

I've broken down these "looks" into specific categories of neighborhoods.

People seem always actually to know with a degree of pain that has required the comfort of fairy tales, that when you are dressed in any particular way at all, you are revealed rather than hidden (Yet the dream that clothes are a disguise has persistently expressed itself in myth and romance.)
—Anne Hollander, *Seeing through Clothes*

Neighborhoods Worldwide

City	I The Establishment	II Newly-arrived	III Eclectic Mix	IV Ethnic enclaves
New York	Carnegie Hill Sutton Place Central Park West Cobble Hill	East 60s-70s Tribeca Upper Riverside Drive	Columbus Ave. East Village- West Village Soho	Little Italy Chinatown
Minneapolis	Wayzata	Edina Eden Prairie	Warehouse District Uptown	Northeast
Los Angeles	Bel Air Hancock Park Los Feliz	Beverly Hills Truesdale Estates	North Hollywood	
Paris	7th, 8th, 16th Arrondissements	6th, 15th, 16th Arrondissements	6th, 10th, 8th Arrondissements	4th, 13th, 20th Arrondissements

Category I: The Establishment

This is a neighborhood I call "The Establishment." It is characterized by people who wear understated, quality clothing and whose homes are furnished with objects which often look as if they had been purchased in the past (and they probably have!). This neighborhood is similar the world over. Each city, however, has its own stamp. In New York City, it's townhouses, brownstones, and turn-of-the century mansions.

In Minneapolis, where I live and work, Wayzata is a Category I neighborhood. It consists of old homes and large estates patterned after English and French architecture, nestled in greenery. The men here have trimly cut hair and wear Establishment clothing—dark blue suits and white shirts. Women wear classic clothing (often shirt-waists), use little makeup, and have simple, neat hairstyles (salon styled or blunt cut). On the weekends, you'll find these inhabitants in top-siders, khakis, and polo shirts.

Category II: The Newly Arrived

This neighborhood is characterized by new money and newly-arrived-at-status. In Minneapolis, suburban Edina reflects this neighborhood. It is a neighborhood reflecting a mixture of the very old and the very latest in architectural design. No tract houses here! The lawns and greenery are more carefully tended, more carefully designed. The men wear slightly longer hair than their Category I counterparts, and while it may look less trim, it is controlled and styled. Suits and accessories are impeccable—well-cut, dark, and prepossessing. Women wear their hair layered or in a cap cut—it's wash 'n wear. Category II women wear the latest fashions, and they dress up to go grocery shopping—generally in sports gear like designer-logoed "sweat" suits, golf outfits, and so on.

Category III: Eclectic Mix

This neighborhood is a creative, eclectic mix. Artists, craftsmen, and intellectuals live here. In Minneapolis, this is the Warehouse District and Uptown. Generally speaking, these neighborhoods tend to be fashionable enclaves in the downtown of major cities where restoration of historical landmarks is the "in" thing. Category III is a mix of the old and new, of low tech and high tech. Men may wear their hair colored and styled with flair. Their clothes further illustrate the eclecticism of their tastes and life styles—Euro-styled suits, deeper hued shirts, and ties that often make a statement. Women here also have carefully colored and styled hair, and they generally like to experiment with design. Their clothes, too, reflect the latest trends and unusual combinations. Both sexes appear to be less "designed," but that is merely an illusion.

Category IV: Ethnic Enclaves

In almost every major city, there are ethnic enclaves which retain elements of the original motherland. You know what I'm talking about: Little Italy in New York; Chinatown in San Francisco; Hamtramack in Detroit; the 13th Arrondissement in Paris. Neighborhoods which change little from generation to generation. Neighborhoods where the young grow up and move out.

If we go to Paris, we can do the same categorizing of neighbor-hoods. And ditto for New York. Los Angeles is a slightly different story because it is sprawled out, making it a bit more difficult to sort out the categories. But they're there.

Indigenous Culture

What you see is that each country, each major city or region, and each neighborhood within those cities has a distinctive "look," a set of meaningful symbols that designate insiders and outsiders, na-tionals and foreigners. No one tells us how to dress or act to fit in. Somehow, we just "know" (we absorb this knowledge of our neigh-borhood, our school, our city, and our culture). And there is no es-caping this "group dress." Because we generally belong to groups, both "group think" and forces outside the group tend to determine our "look."

(Every group in rebellion tries to break out of this "group dress-group think" influence. The hippies of the 60s tried to do this, only to find themselves back in another specific, even more rigid code of dress—so much so that they knew who was serious, who was playing at it, who was doing it to be fashionable, and who were "narcs" in dis-guise. And, like all codes, this one evolved—from jeans to ragged, torn jeans, to strategically patched jeans, to new jeans, tight jeans, and now, back to Lees and Levis—where it all began.)

Clothing "Talks"

. . . the clothing we don calls out, essentially, if not precisely, the same im-ages and associations in ourselves as it does in others, even granted that from time to time and from group to group different values attach to them.
— The Psychology of Fashion

You've heard the phrase, money talks; believe me, clothing talks even louder. You'll readily see that clothing is a strong communica-tor to the outside world. It is carefully, if somewhat unconsciously, orchestrated to send a series of messages. Let's take the theatre as a very strong example of what I am talking about because it graphi-cally illustrates the need to orchestrate these symbols.

When a costume designer and director get together to decide what the characters in the play will wear, they begin by defining the character—his personality, his background, and so on. In a black and white melodrama where there's no question about who is good and who is bad, the choice of clothing (that is, the style, color, shape, and fabric) is pretty simple. The good guys wear white, the bad guys black. The helpless heroine wears white in flowing, curving lines in soft hand fabrics. No man-tailored suit here! The bad girl or woman is stereotypically dressed in red or some other dark color in a revealing decolleté, fanny-tight dress in a shiny fabric. So much for subtlety! Costumes in Shakespearean and other classic plays are as clear: structured dress for rulers, other nobility, and the military; soft, flowing and non-colorful for underlings and peasants. Why these clichés? Because the director wants the audience to immediately identify the actor's character, so there's no guessing or ambivalence. Dress gets directly to the point.

In more complex plays, the rules are a little more complicated but fairly straightforward: dark colors, hard finishes, angular lines for less than good characters. Light colors, soft finishes, refined style in curving lines for vulnerable or heroic characters.

If plays are a little too esoteric, think about some of the old Westerns that were made in Hollywood in the heyday of Westerns. What did Roy Rogers, the Lone Ranger, Gene Autry wear? What did Gary Cooper look like in High Noon? And, conversely, what did the bad guys look like? What did the saloon women look like compared to our heroine Grace Kelly? Today's gangster and hero movies have changed little. The old identification formulas are still valid.

Costumes, as used in the theatre or on the screen, do more than clothes in general—*they act as containers for certain types of behaviors.*

Thus, if costumes, which are representative of behavior, have such power, think of the clothes you wear every day. Like the professional costumer, you need to be aware of what you're doing and what message you're sending. You, too, must orchestrate your dress.

Affluence and Occupation

Just as clothes serve to identify our country of origin and as costumes identify who stands for what, clothing also serves as indicators of position and occupation. While it has always been true that the less affluent have always been differentiated from the affluent, the degree of affluence has not always been clear—except to the *cognoscenti*. In the 17th and 18th centuries, for example, colors, fabric, shapes, and amount and kind of trimming distinguished the affluent. Clearly defined rules existed. Only the nobility for example, could

It is only shallow people who do not judge by appearances. The true mystery of the world is the visible, not the invisible.
— *Oscar Wilde*

Lace was often used as a status symbol. Wealthy families commissioned artisans to make items for their wardrobes and homes. Henry VIII, the English King, passed the Acts of Apparel that no

one under the rank of Knight could wear lace. One pattern was specifically created for the King of Denmark. Only he could wear it. Some countries were so jealous of their patterns that when a country went to war, lacemakers were killed so the patterns wouldn't get into enemy hands. When Louis XIV began to lure Italian lacemakers to France, the Italian government issued a decree—if they didn't return, their next of kin would be jailed and not released until the lacemakers came back or were murdered.
—Marilyn McMahon, *New York Times*

wear six colors at one time. During the reign of Elizabeth I, courtiers wore velvet and satin, scarlet, green, and gold; apothecary's apprentices wore blue cloth coats and a "city cap." Men and women chose their clothing to set them apart from their inferiors; they wanted to keep that distance. Thus, clothing and furnishings were a powerful means of signalling that distance.

Revolutionary Effects

It took the French Revolution to lessen this disparity. The French National Assembly abolished the practice of social distinction by means of dress. The privilege of wearing brocades, feathers, and embroidered clothing was extended to all citizens. After all, how could you have "Liberty, Equality, and Fraternity" if clothing were allowed to separate people? How could men be brothers if the plumage of one was so greatly exaggerated?

Yes, it took political revolution to level the dress of the elite. At first, it was a matter of self-preservation since you could be identified as a member of the nobility by your clothes. Very few dared to display elegance in public: It was simply too dangerous. Yet even when they attempted to disguise themselves by donning peasant dress, they often gave themselves away by their refined demeanor, carriage, and hair). Thus, you were more apt to suffer the guillotine if you sported the trappings of the nobleman. Later, this relaxing of the dress code became a symbol of the new political order in France.

This credo of freedom represented a distinct break between the old and the new. It was exhibited, for instance, in the degree of nakedness permitted. Women began promenading the streets of Paris in transparent muslin over pink silk tights, their bare feet shod in flat-heeled sandals. Another result of this credo is that the dictatorship of men's fashion passed from Paris to across the Channel to London. And thus began the supremacy of London tailoring, particularly on Savile Row.

You can lie in the language of dress just as you can in English, French or Latin, and this sort of deception has the advantage that one cannot be accused of doing it deliberately.
—Alison Lurie, *The Language of Clothes*

This process of levelling was speeded up by the Industrial Revolution. Fussy clothing in easily destroyed fabrics often endangered the safety of the worker. One recalls tales of tragic mishaps in American sweatshops. In the fabric mills, horror stories were rife—women getting their long hair caught in the weaving machines and being scalped before the eyes of coworkers. Limbs of both male and female workers were caught in machinery as a result of voluminous and inappropriate clothing. Something had to be done, and it was. Dress codes were established. *Function ruled.*

Unconsciously, dress began to assume the dull colors and the austerity of the industrial age. This no-nonsense dress was also influenced by self-made men, and it often remains an underlying theme of American business dress today, though at a more sophisticated level.

Here again, there was a differentiation process which accompanied this functionality in dress. Owners, managers, and office workers alike wanted to distinguish themselves from the common laborer. They did so with what has now come to be recognized as the symbols of their position—white collars. These white-collar symbols, which persist today, sent distinct messages: "We don't get dirty." "We can afford to have our clothes laundered often."

And whether it is differentiation for functionality, safety, or status, it is difficult to get away from clothing as a form of separation and identification.

In a more subtle way, however, today's business man is also differentiated from his superiors and from his subordinates. But regardless of position in the company hierarchy, man's dress is the epitome of function. The fit of the suit is such that he can do all that he must in his daily round of business. It is comfortable so that he can move easily about, while at the same time reinforcing his authority. The suit also masks his vulnerability.

Intuitively, we would assume that a positive relationship exists between one's inclination toward fashion in dress and the desire to make an impression through communication. Henry Higgins knew that Eliza Doolittle must both look like and talk like a lady.
—*The Psychology of Fashion*

Power, Status, and Affiliation

To control who wears what, many countries, throughout history, passed sumptuary laws to prescribe or forbid the wearing of specific styles by specific classes of people. In ancient Egypt, for example, only the elite could wear sandals. Ancient Greeks and Romans controlled the type, color, and number of garments worn as well as the type and amount of trimming. During the Middle Ages, almost every aspect of dress was regulated at some place or time. And despite the gains made during and after the French Revolution, laws prescribing dress persisted. In Victorian America, for example, women would have at least six changes of dress per day, and dressing for dinner was *de rigueur* for both sexes. But as class barriers weakened and wealth became more readily attainable, this system of using color and shape to indicate social status began to crumble. What then became the stamp of wealth and rank was the expense of a costume—rich fabrics, superfluous trimmings, and difficult-to-care-for-styles. Until recently, the clothing elegance of a woman—her furs, her jewelry—was a measure of the wealth of her husband or father. (These males, on the other hand, dressed in somber colors and sartorial elegance with little adornment.) One of the biggest changes today is that women buy their own clothes, jewelry, furs, and cars, all reflective of their own wealth, position, and accomplishment.

Who's in Charge?

> Man has from earliest times worn clothes to overcome his feelings of inferiority and to achieve a conviction of his superiority to the rest of creation, including members of his own family, and to win admiration, and to assure himself that he "belongs."
> — Lawrence Langner

While no sumptuary laws operate today, we have little difficulty recognizing who's in charge. I was recently at a luncheon with my two sisters in Dallas. Two of us were dressed rather fashionably. My middle sister was dressed in a traditional navy business suit, white blouse, and understated accessories. When the time came for the check, the waiter, without hesitation, placed it in front of her. Her dress communicated authority (and in this case, my other sister should have been presented the bill).

Lois Fenton, in her book *Dress for Excellence,* tells a similar story about a group of executives at a lunch meeting. The most sartorially, conservatively dressed man in the regulation dark blue suit, white shirt, and rich, silk tie was handed the check. There was no question in the waiter's mind about who was in charge. (Women: Notice how it works when you are out with men. If you haven't arranged for the check beforehand, the man will often be presented with it.)

> Like any elaborate nonverbal language, costume is sometimes more eloquent than the native speech of its wearer. Indeed, the more inarticulate someone is verbally, the more important are the statements made by his or her clothes.
> — Alison Lurie, *The Language of Clothes*

The hierarchy or pecking order in many corporations is clearly defined by symbols which define the level of dress: executive management, senior management, middle management, and supervisory management. This division is sometimes carried out in other nonverbal signals; the more senior the manager, the more he or she consciously or unconsciously is separated from a group. Observe this phenomenon: you will often find senior management walking a little behind the group. If you think I'm exaggerating, just take a look at the management in your organization.

The Uniform

Appropriate clothing serves as a bridge between individuals and signifies insiders, members of the *cognoscenti*. Appropriate clothing, in this case, often means a certain type of uniform. Most of us are aware that a uniform is a series of symbols ordained by the specific culture and adopted by individuals to fit in, signifying that they "belong." No matter how subtle it is, no one is out of uniform.

It happens the day you are born—boys in blue, girls in pink—and despite the current preference for unisex dressing among children, many of us grew up when there were definite differences between clothes for little boys and little girls. Little girls wore pretty dresses in light fabrics and colors which sent the message, "We don't get dirty." Little boys, on the other hand, were dressed in sturdy overalls or jeans and sensible shoes which proclaimed that they were allowed to play rough and they could get dirty. (And despite notions of equality, boys' clothes have always been sturdier and more durable than their female counterparts'. But be aware that a change is in process. Though the world of children is largely unisex, there is more differentiation appearing again. Little girls are back in ruffles, organdy, soft colors, and hair bows).

Teenagers are a wonderful study in the power of the uniform, the power of dress to symbolize belonging. They are the first to adopt fads and fashion, no matter how far out. Today, they have created their own fashion which travels rapidly through schools, groups, cities, and even countries. One of the speediest transmitters between teens in all countries are videos and MTV. These fashions are filled with messages and symbols often designed to irritate or alarm parents, principals, anyone in authority. Generally, this is their first exercise in freedom within the confines of dependency. But sometimes, their choice is a cry for help—a signal that things are getting out of control, that they have fallen in with a troubled group, and, like some in the hippie generation before them, often an alert of drug usage.

Once the uniform is "defined," group acceptance quickly follows. Remember the cashmere "twin" sweater sets of the 40s and 50s? Or the white bucks, chinos, and button-down shirts? Or the first combination adopted by teenage girls—jeans and Dad's white shirt? Or the long hair, sandals, and jeans of the hippie era? Or the citywear (a

Despite their foray onto Seventh Avenue, jeans remain the uniform and essence of the American West. During the 1930s, Easterners vacationing on dude ranches run by farmers impoverished by the Depression, donned jeans and returned home with Western chic. During World War II, jeans manufacturing was deemed an essential industry even though jeans were only purchased by defense workers and were denied the Levi's pocket stitching, characterized as superfluous.

The 1950s heralded Jimmy Dean and Marlon Brando as rebels who were moral, unhypocritical men under their tough, macho, and Levi's exteriors. The mid-1950s also saw adolescents throughout America in jeans. Jeans became the badge of the disillusioned and the discouraged of the 1960s. They were a bond for those under thirty and, to those over thirty, signified the political leanings, the sexual and drug habits, as well as the rebelliousness of the younger generation.

By the 1970s, the baby boomers had begun to turn thirty and to earn middle-class incomes. Along came designer jeans, which gave both status and brand differentiation on the basis of image for the first time.
— *The Psychology of Fashion*

meld of vintage, contemporary, and offbeat laced with punk) of a short time ago?

Even though the "uniform" might be a little more imaginative today, it's still a uniform.

Teenagers around the world are hip to uniforms. (Would you believe I've seen children in a power struggle with their parents over their insistence for a certain brand of shoe/shirt for school). A recent *New York Times Magazine* article described school girls in Milan in their variation of the teenage uniform: "an oversized tweed sport coat borrowed from papa, a demure white blouse with a Peter Pan collar and slim jeans faded to a robin's egg blue topped off by high-top sneakers, clunky Doc Martens shoes, or slightly beat-up Top-Siders."

In New York, teenagers delight in poking fun at the norm—this is one way to stand out from the crowd. A typical look might consist of black stovepipe jeans, an acid green ski jacket, and festoons of gold rope chains. Regardless of where the young live, Patricia Field, owner and operator of the Patricia Field Boutique in Manhattan, quoted in this same article said that what passes for street style varies little from place to place around the world. It's easy to spot the similarities of a teenager in Hong Kong and his or her counterpart in another part of the world.

The whole psychology of the gang is a potent demonstration of uniform and symbol—ranging from the name of the gang to the language and dress to the graffiti they use to mark their turf as well as the insider language, prescribed behaviors, and the tests they must pass to belong. Like the warriors of old, their jeans, leather jackets, and T-shirts are identically decorated. No difficulty in identifying an enemy or outsider.

As we mature and enter the business world, the uniform changes, but is no less important. Generally speaking, the symbols of a man's business uniform are very clear and relatively unchanging. In fact, they haven't changed for over a hundred years. We still find the two piece suit in a fairly limited range of colors, the shirt is a white or blue cotton, the tie a "power" tie in the prescribed color or pattern of the year, and the shoes black or brown. That's it.

The symbols of male uniform are derived from ancient heraldry. Thus, the suit is the vestigial remains of the suit of armor, the vest

. . . the general notion of a *code* . . . means that within contemporary Western culture, a great deal of sign conventionalization obtains in clothing as it does in the arts and crafts generally. Hence, different combinations of apparel with their attendant qualities are capable of registering sufficiently consistent meanings for wearers and their viewers. (In today's world, a tennis outfit will never be mistaken for formal dress or a Nehru jacket for laborer's attire . . . .)
—*The Psychology of Fashion*

a descendant of the coat of mail, and the tie the remains of the heraldic shield, an indicator of whose side you were on, who you were fighting for, and who is the "other side." Is it any wonder, then, that it's a man's world? A world where the symbols are clear, straightforward, and which brook no deviation.

Mixed Signals

For women, however, the symbols are not as clear. Take the case of Ann Hopkins as reported in TIME magazine.

The year is 1978. The place, Washington, D.C. Ann Hopkins is hired as a manager at Price Waterhouse, the Big Eight accounting firm. Four years later, she's nominated for promotion to partnership, the only woman among 88 candidates. During her tenure, Ann managed to bring in between $34 million and $44 million in business and billed more hours the preceding year than any other candidate.

But along the road to her success, it seems that Ann also acquired some negative written evaluations from the firm's partners. They branded her "macho," foulmouthed, and harsh to coworkers. One partner said she should take charm school lessons. The firm put her candidacy on hold for a year. Later, a partner, and one of her biggest supporters, suggested that she might improve her chances if she learned to walk, talk, and dress "more femininely . . . wear makeup, have her hair styled and wear jewelry."

Ann Hopkins left Price Waterhouse and brought suit. She contended that the promotion process violated Title VII of the 1964 Civil Rights Act.

Her plight illustrates the dilemma faced by many professional women who attempt to walk the narrow line between appearing serious and seeming overly severe. "Men in fields that have been long dominated by males tend to expect women to act both feminine and businesslike," says Herma Kay, a sex-discrimination expert at the University of California, Berkeley. "I think they don't realize they're sending out conflicting signals."

Ann Hopkins is not alone in her frustration. Her story illustrates how the right image for the working woman is still unsettled. "Almost anything you wear runs the risk of looking like you're trying to appear just like a man, or too feminine," says University of Miami law school professor Mary Coombs, in the same TIME article.

Businesswomen first imitated men, then they rebelled with an overly feminine style. The current compromise is an Aristotelian mean—a more feminine look, but within clear boundaries. —Dr. Steve Barnett, quoted in *Elle*

Men like to have attractive women on their teams and consider looks as well as capabilities. You fool yourself if you think attractiveness doesn't count. Looks are just as important for men as for women. The way women dress has impact on the way they're viewed as professionals.

The woman who dresses too casually won't be taken seriously, no matter how competent or capable she is. —*NAFE*

A woman who tries too hard to act like a man strikes men as insecure with who she really is. You can be feminine and tough, feminine and a good decision-maker, feminine and command respect.
— NAFE

This dichotomy, I feel, is disappearing. Women's business dress is coming into its own, as witnessed by the clothes of Donna Karan, Ellen Tracy, Perry Ellis, Anne Klein, Calvin Klein, and the Euro-designers—designs which are soft, tailored, *and* female. This "feminization" is accompanied by a new respect for the talents women bring to the workplace—for the way women think. And as more and more women are realizing the power and effectiveness of innately feminine and sensitive behavior, companies have come to realize that this is much healthier for their organizations; more importantly, they recognize that how she behaves works. But it's still an upward battle—even in organizations where this turn-around has occurred—in the face of remarks from some female executives: "It takes a lot of time to be nice."

Rachel Urquhardt, in an article in *Savvy Woman*, writes "There was a time when gleaning people's professions by the clothes they wore was as easy as identifying birds by their plumage. You didn't need field glasses to see the tell-tale markings: the retro-glasses and shredded blue jeans of the MTV warbler; the ugly, chalky, crepe-soled shoes of the white-breasted RN; or the pinstripes and briefcase of the wing-tipped Wall Streeter."

These days, she says, professional plumage isn't quite so easily decoded. "The corporate navy suit with floppy bow tie, the perilously teetering heels of a secretary's pumps, even the penguin-like formality of nuns' habits have faded into a sartorial free-for-all."

Well, not quite!

There is still the persistence that an ill-dressed person, someone who violates the codes established by companies and groups, is probably dishonest, their loyalty is suspect, and they are without talent.

Today, this idea is so well-established that costume historian Anne Hollander, has refused to admit that true virtue can shine through ragged or ugly clothes: "In real life . . . rags [or individuals out of the prescribed uniform] obviously cannot be seen through. . . ."

William Thourlby, in *You Are What You Wear*, maintains that "your appearance is truly the one factor you can control. If you package yourself to manage the impressions you make on others, then their positive reinforcement will, in time, make you the person you want to be. You decide! It's up to you. If you want to be successful—look successful."

Clothes, today and throughout history, are seen as the outward manifestation of inner attitudes, beliefs, and values.

In that way, what Hollander contends is true. If an individual is aware, but doesn't adapt to the proper dress in his or her work environment, we suspect his or her motives, and in many cases, will stop the progress of that individual, will retard his or her marching through our lives, through our organizations.

The question of image is not a superficial one. A poor image is a barrier that must be overcome, and can be, once personality and skills become apparent. But why set up the barrier in the first place?
—"The Professional Image Report," *Working Woman*

If you want to move up in the organization, you go along with the culture. If you don't care, well, you can wear anything.

—Cora Rose, Manager, IBM

2
Deciphering the Code

Webster's New Collegiate Dictionary defines culture as "the integrated pattern of human behavior that includes thought, speech, action, and artifacts and depends on man's capacity for learning and transmitting knowledge to succeeding generations." In business, this definition translates to "the way we do things around here."

The "way we do things around here" I call corporate culture. Often mysterious and unknown to the outsider, it can also be elusive and constricting to the insider. But nevertheless it is real, whether an articulated artifact or something that is "in the air." Corporate culture is as real and as imprinting as the culture of a nation; it's also as protective and rule-laden as any family.

Every business and every organization has a culture. Sometimes it is fragmented and difficult to perceive from the outside. Sometimes it is strong and cohesive. Regardless of its strength or weakness, culture is the backdrop for everything that goes on in an organization. It affects areas such as:

- who gets the promotion and how they got it
- how and what decisions to make
- who can, and when can they, make changes without "making waves"
- the language spoken
- how employees dress

In the real world, a great man will overcome any superficiality of appearance, any deficiencies of dress. But executives on the rise may be judged by their dress more than those who have already reached the top.
—Stanley Marcus, quoted in *Dress for Excellence*

A company's environment determines what a company must do to be successful and is perhaps the single greatest influence in shaping its culture. In their book, *Corporate Cultures*, Terrance Deal and Allan Kennedy suggest that companies which sell undifferentiated products have one kind of culture—a work hard, play hard culture, while companies which have an R & D focus have a "bet your company future" culture. Imbedded in the culture are the beliefs and values which define success (whether team playing, grandstanding, or supporting others) in concrete terms for employees. It says to us, if you do this you will be successful.

Because every organization has its own culture, these tactics and strategies are unique. Even in the same industry, cultures are different. In the high tech industry, for example, IBM is seen as understated, efficient, neat, and tidy. But a Cray Research or an Apple Computer, on the other hand, is seen as loose, creative, messy, and ambiguous.

Every organization has its heroes. These are individuals who personify the culture's values, who are role models for the rest of the organization. In some companies, heroes are born; in others, they are made. Heroes are those who have gone the extra mile, who have made strong contributions that ultimately have symbolic impact. And people love telling stories about these heroes.

C. Brooklyn Derr, in his book *Managing the New Careerist*, tells this story about one of his clients. At a small chemical company, every executive had a truck driver's hard hat as part of the office decor. The reason: "At one point in the company's history, the truck drivers had worked around the clock for about a ten-day stretch, delivering explosives to save a mining contract of such crucial importance that the company might have gone under without it." Truck drivers were the company's heroes.

Another factor which makes up a corporate culture is its rites and rituals; in other words, the routines of everyday life which show employees the kind of behavior expected. Often, how people behave carries more impact than what a company "says." In companies where the culture is strong, they "dictate" exactly how they want their employees to behave. They go so far as to spell out the acceptable decorum and the expectations clients and insiders have. They define procedures and processes which are the mundane rites and rituals on how "we do things around here." In strong cultures, no event is too trivial to be managed.

Deal and Kennedy contend that companies with strong cultures "take pride in the way they do things and work hard to make sure that way is right. They regard the carrying out of activities in the correct way as tangible examples of the strength of the culture." They give an example from that exemplar of strong culture, IBM: "You'll never see IBM salespeople along with the hordes of others congregating at Howard Johnson's [for breakfast] every morning, because IBMers are encouraged to see their time as too valuable to waste in a roadside diner. When IBMers want coffee they will share it with a client or colleague. . . . [they] begin the day . . . by focusing on the company, the industry, and their habits as professionals."

Rites and rituals, Deal and Kennedy further suggest, guide behavior in corporate life and are, "in effect, dramatizations of the company's basic cultural values. . . . Rituals provide the place and script with which employees can experience meaning; they bring order to chaos." In addition, they govern everything from meetings (the number held per month, where they're held and who is invited to attend, starting time, who sits where, even to the kind or shape of table) to language standards, public decorum, interpersonal behavior, and presentation standards.

Culture: An organization's heart

The heart of any organization is its culture. It dictates everything from the corporate logo to the dress of its personnel, from the top on down. Just how is this culture communicated? Written or unwritten, everything an organization does, everything an organization is, stems from its cultural biases. And these biases are communicated very strongly through an organization's people. In some cases, culture is an unwritten set of norms which is communicated by behavior more than by formal rules. Even more importantly, these are communicated on a gut level; in other words, you just know that something does or does not feel right.

Let's take a look at three wonderful examples of organizational culture.

Ross Perot's EDS*

Flexibility. Recognizing and rewarding people. Teams which operated like a band of guerrillas. Performance. Loyalty. Trial and error. Tolerance of mistakes. Do what's right for the customer. Make money. Results. Listen to the troops. Get in the trenches.

These are the attitudes, beliefs, and values which were representative of Electronic Data Systems (EDS), the company founded by "cowboy capitalist" H. Ross Perot. In other words, a culture which honored the man in the field and encouraged him to make his own decisions, regardless of his title or his position in the hierarchy. But to outsiders, EDS looked like a military compound—there were fences and guards surrounding the complex, flags, clean shaven men in white shirts, dark suits, shined shoes, and army haircuts. One EDS veteran compared it to a tank: "Put it in low gear, and it could run over everything." Another said, "Our gunner's command was simple. Ready, aim, fire, fire, fire, fire, fire."

EDS, a strong culture which inspired the loyalty of insiders and the fear and dislike of outsiders, so much so that when Perot sold EDS to General Motors (GM) the clash of cultures was such that GM people labeled EDS employees "corporate moonies and Perotbots." But EDS staffers didn't care; they *knew* they were right.

Perot Systems*

While most companies don't set down the "rules of the culture," Perot Systems believes it's imperative to make such a statement—to make sure recruits know what they were getting into. Perot says, "These principles and philosophies are so direct and so specific they might cause you to join or not to join, but you wouldn't wonder three or four years later what the philosophies were." So what does this culture look like? What values will be rewarded? Let's take a look at the operating principles Perot Systems enforces.

*From an article in INC., "The Cowboy Capitalist"

At Perot Systems, "they will:

- Have only one class of team member—each member will be a full partner.
- Recognize and reward excellence while the individual is still sweating from his efforts.
- Build and maintain a spirit of 'one for all and all for one.'
- Encourage every team member to take risks, make decisions, exercise initiative, and never be afraid to make mistakes.
- Hold team members accountable for results, with . . . great flexibility in deciding how to achieve results [and] the clear understanding that ethical standards must never be compromised.
- Eliminate any opportunity for people to succeed by merely 'looking good.'
- Promote solely on merit."

Furthermore, "Perot Systems will not tolerate anyone who:

- Discriminates against another. . . .
- Looks down on others.
- Becomes a corporate politician.
- Tries to move ahead at the expense of others.
- Takes illegal drugs."

3M: Masters of Innovation*

Wide tolerance for new ideas. Belief that unfettered creative thinking pays off in the end. Scarcity of corporate rules. Tolerance of failures. Informal information-sharing sessions. Self-policing. Is big but acts small. Divisional autonomy. The whole greater than the sum of its parts.

3M, a major manufacturer of industrial and consumer products in St. Paul, Minnesota, which encompasses some 100 new businesses or new major product lines over the last 60 years, interestingly, relies on a few simple rules:

- Keep divisions small. Know staffers' first names.
- Tolerate failure, thereby increasing the chances for new product hits.

*From an article in Business Week, "Masters of Innovation"

- Motivate the champions. Product idea people have a chance to run their own product group or division.
- Stay close to the customer. Routinely invite customers in to brainstorm product ideas.
- Share the wealth.
- Don't kill a project. Provide seed money for new product ideas.

And the credo of 3M's spiritual founder, William L. McKnight, is still operative today: "If management is intolerant and destructively critical when mistakes are made, I think it kills initiative." A credo which a current article in *Business Week* says "breeds loyalty and management stability."

3M, a culture where anyone can succeed, where "daydreaming" is permissible, even encouraged. 3M, a "highly responsive laboratory and development partner . . . known for its commitment to quality and an uncommon willingness to experiment and innovate." A company where, say Japanese management experts Ikujiro Nonaka and Tatsuo Kiyosawa, in their book, *The Challenge of 3M: Managing Creativity*, "low-ranking research and manufacturing workers, even marketing employees, can bring up development ideas."

The Code of Corporate Culture

In most companies, rules or cultural dictates are not specifically written down. They are unspoken. They are communicated to the newcomer through role models, through promotion patterns, through the daily carrying out of business. But whether they're written or unwritten, they determine the image a company projects to its stakeholders: its employees, its community, its shareholders, its customers.

Although there are distinctive cultures like the Perot EDS (prior to its sale to GM), Perot Systems, and 3M in all industries and companies, there are distinctive traits or cultural norms in every organization. How do you go about defining yours if it's not written down? Derr suggests you find the answers to the following questions.

- What legacy did the company's founders leave?

For example, a strong leader like Herbert Marcus of Neiman-Marcus left a strong imprint on his retail business. His son, Stanley Marcus, echoing his father in what has become the Neiman-Marcus

This morning he was a serious individual, representing Park Avenue and Wall Street. He wore a blue-gray nailhead worsted suit, custom-tailored in England for $1,800, two-button, single-breasted, with ordinary notched lapels, half-brogued New and Lingwood shoes with the close soles and the beveled insteps. . . . On Wall Street double-breasted suits and peaked lapels were considered a bit sharp . . .
—Tom Wolfe, *The Bonfire of the Vanities*

"Golden Rule," says "There is never a good sale for Neiman-Marcus unless it is a good buy for the customer."

- Who are the heroes? Who are the deviants (those who dare to "push" the culture)?

A perfect example of heroes are the truck drivers previously mentioned.

- What is the company folklore—the legends and myths—that affects the way things are done?
- What do you have to do to get ahead? To make it to the top?

Study precedents and case histories. Learn from mentors, colleagues, and sponsors.

- Which group is dominant—engineers, managers, marketeers? Which unit wields the greatest power?
- What are the taboos of your culture?
- What are the norms about time?
- Is there a corporate sport? More than one? Are they important?
- What are the visible symbols (lapel pins, blazers, gold pens, etc.) that are important?
- What is the organizational language? What are the current "buzzwords"?

For example, are conversations sprinkled with terms from sports, the army, or the navy?

- What are the culture-sustaining rituals (picnics, managerial retreats, meeting rituals)?
- What is the dress code and how important is it?

The Right Signals

Business clothes always say something. They do not necessarily tell others who you are as a person, but they do signal what or who you represent. Just as you would harbor doubts about the competence of a bricklayer who arrived on the job site in dress slacks or about the bedside manner of a doctor in T-shirt and sandals, you undoubtedly have expectations about the appearance of your lawyer, your accountant, your broker. Perhaps, even more important, you have expectations about the dress of your colleagues, your subordinates, and the individuals you answer to in whatever field you are in.

Fashion is a mode of symbolic expression—a clue to sexual identity, socialization, culture, status, age, occupational role, personality, mood, and possibly communicator style.
— *The Psychology of Fashion*

Expectations are so strong, and so true to form, that it is possible to accurately guess that this individual is an accountant, that this one is from New York, this one is in design. The signs, the code, are so strong that most individuals adapt to them. Some do so consistently, deliberately; others unconsciously; but regardless of how it's done, they are signalling that they are part of a group or organization and that they are committed to acting in accordance with the norms, standards, and goals of their peers.

Frequently, this assimilation happens unconsciously. Newcomers don't even know how they have assimilated the dress code and behavior. If, for example, one man in the office puts his jacket on the back of a chair, that action is probably a clue that most, or all, do. If, on the other hand, a top executive puts it on a hanger on the back of the door, you'll soon see everyone doing it. In some companies, work is done with the jacket on; in still others, taking the jacket off means getting down to business. It signals "do not disturb" or "men at work." Ken Kelly, an attorney with New York's Epstein Becker, says that at his firm, most of the lawyers work jacketless in their offices, even when they are meeting with clients. It's not an uncommon sight, he emphasizes, to have a working session with senior partners — with everyone in shirtsleeves.

There are some, however, who can get away with being different as they dress against the norm. John Jay, whom you met earlier, says that his style of dress is "really part of breaking the rules." A result, he theorizes, of either "being Asian and going into the arts, or just wanting to break the rules." And breaking the rules is part of working at Bloomingdale's, New York's fabled fashion department store, which encourages creativity in its design people to do something different.

Jim Binger, former chairman and chief executive of Minneapolis' Honeywell and now owner of Jujamcyn, a Broadway organization with five New York theatres, has straddled both the corporate world and the artistic world. He says that though clothes don't matter, when they are extreme or far from the norm of the prevailing culture, clothes make a difference. No matter how talented the individual — engineer or playwright — it's still hard to trust in that talent when the individual pays too little attention to his appearance. Talent may win in the end, but it will take a lot more work and a lot

Style, in clothing as elsewhere, is a combination of personal expression and social norms. . . . Clothing occupies a special place, as the manner of communication which is closest, metaphorically and literally, to the self. It covers what is to be private and shows the world the presentation a person wants to make.
— *The Psychology of Fashion*

In the business world it is essential to understand the coded messages that clothing and color signal.
— Jacqueline Murray

longer for the nonconforming individual's ideas to be accepted, a lot longer for others to trust that talent.

Defining the Dress Code

Dress codes may be as defined as the one described above for EDS, the organizational look of an IBM, or as loosely defined as those at an RCA Records. But whichever it is, every company has a code. If you can't recognize it in your current company, take a look at another company in your industry. Often, it's easier to spot the signs from the outside. In any organization, people know how to dress appropriately, even when the dress is (Heaven forbid!) rumpled polyester. Either they conform to what is acceptable and, in effect, accept the culture or they rebel by wearing clothes that are slightly out of sync, and thereby signal their rebellion.

I remember working with a major Midwestern bank several years ago. The executive ranks of this bank preferred a narrow, four-in-hand knot for ties; one of their officers tied his necktie in a Windsor knot. (The Windsor knot was part of the old guard, and the four-in-hand came in with new management.) This subtle difference signalled to his fellow officers that the man was not totally happy. His refusal to accept the four-in-hand knot was symptomatic of his resistance to changes in the bank's rules and regulations. In effect, he was proclaiming himself a stonewaller, a rebel.

Just as clothing signals rebellion or acceptance, if it is not chosen carefully, it can send the wrong signals.

I worked with the wife of a computer engineer who was developing a sleek style of business dress. Her husband decided to follow suit and before long, he was being courted for a management position at his firm. His colleagues kept saying, "You're ready to move up; you're management material." But his wife told me that he liked being an engineer and wanted no part of management. In this particular case, the engineer had to reassess the message he was broadcasting with his new wardrobe. Did he want to be a part of management, or was he more comfortable with engineers and being an engineer? Whatever his decision, he had to dress appropriately. And in that particular environment, he would have to go back to "engineer dress" for management to leave him alone.

Admirals and generals have their medals, gold stripes, ribbons, stars and bars to signify rank. The business world, too, responds to power signals, but subtler ones.
—Working Woman

Clothes do not make the man, but they are a way of stating his value codes. If you are dealing in a scarce commodity like money, appearances are a guide to the mind-set—the values—of the person you are conversing with.
—George L. Ball, quoted in *Dress for Excellence*

Let me give you another example of the power of the code.

A young computer programmer interested in dressing well came to me for advice. I suggested he check out the dress norms at his firm. He did so with an executive several levels above him who said, "Sure, if it'll help you do your job." After he made his "new" dress changes, he became aware of the discomfort of his peers. They joked about it. Some were actually hostile. He was amazed, however, that many executives greeted him in the halls of the company—those very same executives who had never "seen" him before. The difference? He was now wearing their symbols. They recognized him as an "insider." And part of that particular message is that if you're not wearing the right symbols, you're invisible to certain levels in the organization.

Individuals respond toward objects on the basis of the meanings these objects hold for them.
— The Psychology of Fashion

All companies apply some version of the standard dress code for business in general as well as some specific signatures. For example, the navy suit, white shirt, and red tie of IBM executives are the signatures which identify the insiders—not only to themselves, but to the outside world as well.

Deal and Kennedy suggest, for example, that "tough guy" cultures are " 'in fashion' all the time; the stars of the culture often make a real effort to look different from their peers—but not too different. If everyone else has a Gucci briefcase, the star will come in with a Mark Cross briefcase. Pretty soon everyone else will have one too, then the game begins again. Worker/players on the other hand, avoid extremes of dress, choosing instead to stay with the norms of middle America—sports jackets, plaids, shirt sleeves, and in the computer companies, jeans. Bettors [those involved in R & D companies who bet on the future] and process people are conservative dressers, and what they wear tends to coincide with their rank. Junior people look like junior people. The higher ranks often appear in dark, three-piece suits."

A close look at clothes and fashion gives us an opportunity to understand other human beings even beyond their outward appearance.
— The Psychology of Fashion

In spite of these "obvious" symbols, I know that many companies are not aware of their own codes and even tell me that they have no dress code. When I ask employees and management about their code, about their symbols, they can't enumerate them; yet they all exhibit a "company look."

This "look" transcends industries and cultures and translates into three categories: Corporate, Communicator, and Creative.

Category I	Category II	Category III	

Category I

Corporate Dress

Banking
Accounting
Law
Fortune 500
  companies
Traditional
  companies

Category II

Communicator

Sales
Marketing
Education
Personnel
Real Estate
Medical
Establishing
  companies

Category III

Creative

Interior Design
Retail
Advertising
Commerical Art
Entrepreneurial
  companies

*Categories
at a
Glance*

I Upper
    management
  Accounting
  Legal

II Personnel
  Marketing
  Sales
  People Managers

III Advertising
   Public Relations

*Jobs
Within Each
Category*

Category I   **Category II**   **Category III**

*Interaction
Between
Categories*

3

Category I:
Corporate Dress

Corporate, or Category I, dressing is representative of Fortune 500 companies. These are companies with a traditional, conservative culture where being team players is *de rigueur*. Here, corporate dress is the most structured and formal of the three variations. Large corporations, law firms, banks, and accounting firms which make up Category I tend to be traditional and predominantly male. (The mix at these firms is changing steadily; women are consistently filling out the ranks, and with time and experience will keep moving into higher and higher levels.) All have deeply entrenched dress codes which are, quite frankly, impossible to buck.

Hallmarks of the Culture

What are some of the hallmarks of the culture? To begin with, there are clear, strict rules of behavior characterized by layers of hierarchy, reporting structures, and protocols. Category I companies value discipline, order, and efficiency. It's a very left-brain environment where logic and linear solutions are applauded and change takes place incrementally.

If you were to walk around a Category I organization, you would find it to be quiet and subdued. This atmosphere carries through on corporate logos, building design, office configurations, and so on. Nothing is wasted in this environment—there is no excess of paper, communication, or of movement. Why gesture wildly when one single telling gesture will do? There's a certain economy in Category I companies. They have arrived at the success patterns that are replicable, and everything they do conforms to those patterns.

Category I individuals do business with a quiet efficiency; they are no nonsense, fact-oriented people. They are highly verbal rather than highly visual; numbers and non-subjective data are the basis for decision making. Fortune 500 companies like IBM, American Express and its subsidiaries, Citibank, General Dynamics, Bank of America, accounting firms, the major national and international investment banking houses, as well as the giant, old-line "Wall Street" law firms are all traditional, conservative companies. It is safe to say that most of these Fortune 500s will generally fall between Categories I and II.

The following chart summarizes Category I dress characteristics.

Corporate dress is the most structured and formal of the three major variations of business dress. As such, it is the uniform worn by the more traditional and conservative businesses:

Category I: Corporate

- Banking
- Accounting
- Law
- Fortune 500 companies
- Phase 2 companies

Dress in this category is characterized as follows:

	Shape	Color	Fabric
Business Suits and Dresses	Simple line, shape, and design	Gray, dark blue Subtle experimentation with colors that blend well in a conservative environment	Herringbone Tweed Subtle pattern mixes Silk Nailshead Flannel
Blouses and Shirts	Tailored Simple line and design Softly pleated and gathered Open-neck/lapel	White Off-white Geometric prints Multi-colors	Cotton Wool Challis Voile Linen

Uniforms. The word connotes something sedate or straitlaced, but the uniform is simply an attitude toward dressing. It's the kind of thing you want to wear more than once a week—a combination of pieces that look all of a piece. It's a solution: you don't have to think about making a look work—it already does.
— Mirabella

In Category I, it's important to pay close attention to all elements of the basic uniform. For men, it's dark suits, tie shoes, conservative ties, and white or blue shirts. (You might even see some lightly striped shirts, part of London's impact in this globalization of business.) For women, it's matched suits in solid colors or subtle patterns. Blouses, like the male shirt, are white, off white, or in colors that are lighter than the suit, often in silk. The skirts that work best are straight and worn slightly below the knee. In Category I, dresses are not generally worn without a jacket, except by women who are high up in management (as the apparel industry improves on its dress fashions, more and more women today are welcoming dresses into their business wardrobes).

But whether you're male or female, quality counts here, and it's often the distinguishing mark between higher and lower echelons. Category I dress codes are more implicit than explicit. You observe who's wearing what and then emulate the best. The code also varies the least from city to city and region to region. A banker in New York will look pretty much like a banker in San Francisco.

At FYI, a personal wardrobe and shopping service of the Dayton-Hudson organization, over thirty percent of the clients work for Category I companies. And while the clothing choices may seem, to the outsider, hopelessly limiting, it is important to remember that the individuals who inhabit these professions and organizations are comfortable with their tried and true formulas which yield predictably positive results. It's part of the innate practicality that is exhibited by persons who choose that work and that culture. In addition, a woman knows there is a fine, but definite, line between business design and fashion. Category I organizations are less tolerant than any other Category of dress—they see the lack of precision as "less right." (The chart on the preceding page provides guidelines for Category I dressing.)

The men and women on the following pages are extremely successful people who know what it takes to succeed in Category I organizations. Here, they share their thoughts and insights about the culture as well as their personal styles. They know it takes appreciation of the cultural norms as well as the development of a personal style. They illustrate that even in this most formal and structured of categories, individuality is possible, nay, even desirable.

The way we dress is a personal signature. The dress or suit we wear is not just a confirmation of the old adage that "Clothes make the man," but rather an example of the fact that our individuality is expressed largely in the way we dress.
— The Psychology of Fashion

Bob Kase
managing director

"I come from a family in Brooklyn who didn't know where Wall Street was, let alone what it was." Making his own way has been a *sine qua non* for Bob Kase, Managing Director-Syndicate for Furman Selz Mager Dietz & Birney Incorporated in New York. "I began as a file clerk doing temp work at L. F. Rothschild while working my way through graduate school. I didn't have the right background, the right education, or the right connections, so the best thing that I could sell was *me*." Kase learned "by osmosis" and created a niche for himself that has carried him from file clerk to top executive.

His individuality, his "gift for gab," his people skills, and his knack for fitting the role make Kase stand out in a crowd. "After Rothschild's went under, I had to depend on myself. I got a new lease on life and came up with my own "shtick." I don't want to be part of the masses, so I capitalize on my individuality."

In defining his personal style, Kase eschews the standard conservative blue suit with cuffs and opts for one of European flair. He likes European suits (some of his favorites are Hugo Boss, Bill Kaisermann, and Armani), Italian loafers, interesting socks, and unique ties. "You can get great ties for $5.00 on the Lower East Side. I don't care about labels. I just like to look good and feel good in it. Wall Street has changed in many ways from years ago," Kase states. "Years ago, you had to go to Choate, and it was taboo to wear brown."

The vigorous entrepreneurial culture of Furman Selz bypasses those earlier hide-bound attitudes. "Our departments are very autonomous, but they meld. Within the hierarchy we let people do what works." The firm is 20 - 25 percent women and continues to generate consistent revenues. "While other firms are folding, we're building up."

As the first member of his family to go to college, Kase has really made it on his own. His advice for others who want to advance: "Always be clean, shoes polished, fingernails trimmed, hair neat. Buy a couple of good pieces and take care of them. Add style with shirts or ties. Dress the way the role expects, but try to be an individual."

"I guess you could call me a "Gatsby of shirts"; I don't buy when I need I buy when I see."

Juanita Costa
vice president

From the time she was a teacher of textiles and fashion to her position as a top executive at IDS, Juanita Costa has always been cognizant of the importance of dress. "I truly believe clothing, in many ways, is a costume. You can use clothing to help you, personally and professionally. People often do it without realizing it, but you adopt the costume of the job you want."

Costa began her career as a professor of textile science, got her MBA in finance at Boston University, spent several years on Wall Street, and now happily resides in Minneapolis where she is Vice President of Pooled Investments for IDS. Costa sees marked differences between New York business style and Midwest dress. "New York is much more fashionable, by and large. Business women in New York are wearing designer clothes in an understated fashion.

They favor natural fibers in tailored suits and dresses, in a relaxed style (softer fabrics, softer lines), still very business-like, but it's not the 'power suit.' In contrast, Midwestern women often feel they must still 'look like a man,' in dark suits, cotton shirts and ties. That look left New York about five years ago."

Availability is one of the problems Costa sees in the Midwest marketplace. "You can buy wonderful casual clothes here, but not the good quality, mid-priced $300-$500 suit. I have to do all my business shopping in Chicago and New York. It's very frustrating." Costa has maintained her sophisticated New York look since moving to the Midwest. She finds she gets a lot of comments and has noticed that women on her staff are following her lead in their wardrobe selection since her arrival. "I believe in not buying anything unless it's exceptional. That's how I shop."

"Women want to look different; they don't want to look the same."

High visibility is key in Costa's work. Her main business contacts are clients for whom she puts together investment packages. She describes the culture at IDS as "a treasure. There is much more concern for the family and quality of life here and throughout the Midwest that you just don't see in the East. It's much healthier." She thrives under IDS's emphasis on team effort, excellence, and commitment to clients.

In her client meetings, unlike many businessmen and women, Costa does not tailor her look for a particular client. She stays consistent with her personal role and style. "I have a very professional look. Very tailored, but soft and feminine. I wear suits in a variety of subtle colors and patterns. I even have a red suit! I find that I am buying more dresses now. But I definitely reflect a business look all the time."

*Teresa M. Holland
and Kenneth J.
Kelly, attorneys*

Teresa M. Holland and Kenneth J. Kelly are attorneys at the twelve-year old New York based lawfirm Epstein Becker. Coming from diverse professional backgrounds, Holland and Kelly are comfortable with the vigorous entrepreneurial, un-stuffy culture at Epstein Becker. Individual assertiveness is encouraged and individual style is accepted, within bounds, of course. "For example, here I can wear red nail polish or a red jacket, but I would never at the firm I worked for previously," Holland comments.

As attorneys, Holland and Kelly are fully aware of the psychological powers of clothing and use it to their advantage — to impress, to put at ease, to say "we mean business." Although he never wears a jacket in his office, Kelly will put on one to meet a client for the first time. He'll then take it off during the meeting because he feels this relaxes the client. Holland always wears her jacket during a deposition because "It's just like being in court." When preparing for a case, Kelly will check out the style of the client company and dress accordingly. At trial, Kelly and Holland manipulate their look to convey subtle messages to the jury. On the first day: dark blue suit, white shirt — conservative, serious. After a day or two to build empathy — more relaxed look: lighter suit, blue shirt. Third day: light grey suit, light shirt and tie. Summation: return to the serious, more formal look of day one.

"Dress can provide a tactical advantage."

Although less prescriptive, than, say, a Wall Street firm or an investment banking firm, there is definitely a "New York lawyer look." It's a conservative, high quality, city look with a slightly wider range of colors and textures. When Kelly was the only New York lawyer at a trial in New Jersey, the judge commented, "You're from New York, aren't you."

Women have a much less clearly defined look since they are a fairly recent addition to the legal profession. Holland's career has run the gamut, beginning in civil rights and government work in the early 70s when she and her colleagues wore jeans at the office. As she moved into private practice, she knew she needed to cultivate a more professional look, but the only senior woman she saw was a "tough older woman who wore floral shirt dresses, short hair, and no make-up."

Now, Holland opts for a coordinated suit, avoids looks that are too trendy or too fixed-up, and the ultimate *coup de grâce*, looking provocative. "The worst thing a woman can do in a professional setting is look over dressed. Wearing sexy clothes is unthinkable. It puts you into a 'merely ornamental' rank." To succeed in a culture primarily defined by men, many women have adopted the man-tailored suit and tie in order to compete. Holland notes that some female professionals are now moving away from the "bow tie brigade" to a softer more individual look.

On the international scene, Kelly sees differences. "All women in France look provocative; it's part of their culture. They know how to dress." He feels, however, that the British woman does not have the same flair, commenting that "even a good looking woman in London can make herself unattractive."

*Fred Gaines
attorney*

Entertainment lawyer Fred Gaines, a man of discretionary taste in business and clothing, characterizes himself as "a catalyst, a partner, in his clients' lives."

In the seventies, Gaines started a firm that grew into a powerhouse of forty-plus lawyers and found himself doing too much business administration and not enough lawyering. He didn't like it. "Here, at Mayer, Glassman & Gaines, we're very selective. We have twelve lawyers, and we work very hard. We choose our clients carefully. Although we're small, we consider ourselves one of the preeminent firms in the city in entertainment law. We're a boutique, not a department store. We specialize."

With a very broad client base, from sophisticated businessmen to "rag tag" musicians, from large companies to individual performers, Gaines characterizes his firm as friendly, bright, and animated, with "a certain spark of energy."

There is no dress code among the attorneys at the firm. "We're a boutique. Part of what a boutique's about is individuality rather than too much of the same." Most of the male attorneys at the firm dress in suits. "I probably dress more casually than anyone else in the office. I prefer sport coats." The female attorneys in the firm, as well as two of the partners and two of the male associates, wear very sophisticated business clothing. The staff looks a bit more casual, less polished, but still businesslike.

Dress choices vary slightly according to agenda. For a court appearance or a meeting with a banker, most of the office would dress a bit more formally, a darker suit, or a stripe rather than a tweed. Gaines says that when he travels to the East coast, to Europe, and to Australia on business, he tailors his clothing more to weather demands rather than who he's seeing. "If I go to New York or Europe in the winter I can wear wools and tweeds that I can't wear here." He might take along a dress suit or a tuxedo may accompany him if the occasion arises.

"I think presentation is essential to success. You want your clients to have confidence in you and see you as competent. They may need to lean on you in a difficult time." Gaines looks for that extra sparkle in his people and cultivates it in his firm. "You've got to have that client contact, and your appearance influences opinions."

"Lawyering is a lot of things. It's lots of things about what you are—and dress is important."

Beverly Chalfen
president

Beverly Chalfen is always gracious, cultured, and very feminine, no matter which of her several professional "hats" she's wearing. Her career involvements range from president of a bank holding company, part-owner of "Holiday on Ice," chair for the Donor Relations Committee for the Minnesota Orchestra, to board member of the St. Paul Chamber Orchestra, the Children's Theatre Company of Minneapolis, Mount Sinai Hospital, and the new Minneapolis Convention Center Plaza.

With her wide agenda of business, social, and philanthropic activities, across the United States and abroad, Beverly has a wardrobe that ranges from very casual, to businesslike, to elegant evening wear. She has an innate fashion sense, of blending perfectly into each setting—business or social—while retaining her own refined sense of style. She is *always* appropriate.

There's a pithy anecdote about Beverly which graphically illustrates her fashion expertise. She was at a gathering in the Twin Cities recently and everyone was in a dither about what to wear to the grand opening of the new Saks Fifth Avenue. A friend turned to her and said, "Beverly you're the only one here who would not only know

what to wear, but have it [in your closet]. . . . " Beverly sees clothing as art, part of the entire ambiance of a scene.

In her own organization (The First National Banks of Anoka and
Brooklyn Park), she cultivates this feeling of fitting in with the environment. "It's in a nice neighborhood and is very community-
minded. People are fairly conservative, clean-cut Midwestern, and
very friendly." Although she's a personal fan and collector of modern
art, she says she "would never put some huge Picasso in the lobby.
It wouldn't be suitable." Chalfen's sense of graciousness and warm
openness plays a steady, strong part in influencing her bank personnel, and she sees her role as one of bringing the positive aspects of
femininity to her business. "Women are open. They're listeners. We
bring the capacity to nurture to the business world."

Expressing this softness is part of her wardrobe guidelines. "I wear
a tailored style, but very soft. I always include a bow or some pearls
to say 'I'm a woman.' I want to convey an image of inner strength
while being non-abrasive and non-threatening. I love being a
woman."

"Women are open. They're listeners."

*Fletcher Wright
managing partner*

"Open, direct, participative, action-oriented, and service-directed" is how Deloitte & Touche's managing partner Fletcher Wright describes this Big Six accounting firm. "We're what you call 'auditors' auditors.' We provide technical and business seminars world wide."

"At Deloitte & Touche," he says, "there's a strong ethic for doing things right — and in the best possible way for clients. A service orientation is really the driver — we take pride in giving value-added service."

To do this, the company hires the very best people. "Then," Fletcher adds, "we give them lots of flexibility. There are guidelines, of course, and there are expectations, but how they get there is less important. There's a delicate balance between individual goals and the strategic direction of the firm."

Flexibility seems to be the key to the success of this international organization. It extends from a culture which espouses teamwork and value added service to the dress of its employees. The older partners, for example, wear jackets all the time, even when working in the privacy of their offices. "I'm less formal, generally," Fletcher says. "I don't wear a jacket. But I do dress to fulfill my clients' expectations."

"I guess you'd have to say that we do not impose a dress code. We expect our people to be well-dressed and well-groomed. This is the norm among the Big Six. Regionals and locals may differ, but there is a certain interchangeability. We're not distinctively dressed; we look much the same as the people at the other firms." If there is a distinctive characteristic, Fletcher would attribute it more to the socio-economic level of his employees. Accountants are in an upper income bracket and can afford to dress better.

Of his own style, he says, "I sport a tasteful executive appearance — well-dressed, but not showy. Conservative but impressive." His wardrobe consists of the traditional American cut suit, mostly in gray and variations of gray. For example, the day he was interviewed he was wearing a subtle gray windowpane plaid, a blue silk tie, and pink pocket square.

Surprising to this transplanted Southerner is the fact that "Atlanta is more conservative in dress than Minneapolis." He also notes that women in the business are dressing better and seem to be conscious of dressing in a professional arena. "Here at Deloitte & Touche," he says, "we see a fair number of suits and the higher up in the organization, the more dresses we see."

Deloitte & Touche, like many organizations in the late 80s, is making a concerted effort to hire more women. "Our present recruiting plan calls for us to include fifty per cent women in the new hires."

What dress advice would he give to those beginning their careers? "First," he says, "make sure you have good taste in what you select. Secondly, err on the side of spending too much. After all, you get what you pay for. Third, if you have any doubts, get guidance, and lastly, learn by association what is acceptable."

Manager of Cost Accounting Services for IBM in Poughkeepsie, New York, Cora Rose is the highest ranking woman at her facility. The epitome of corporate culture, IBM is a model of the conservative, "team-playing" company. Although there is no written dress code, there is definitely a "uniform," consisting of a blue suit, white shirt, and red tie. Rose sees this as "purely a matter of good business sense. If you want to move to the next level, then you dress as the next level does. That really is the culture."

*Cora Rose
manager*

The same code applies for both men and women. Women who want to be taken seriously in this corporate climate steer away from bright colors, patterns, frilly blouses, and dresses. Rose rarely wears dresses, and when she does, "only a shirtwaist that I can wear with a jacket." Most of the time, however, she dons the traditional two piece suit and cotton shirt. She describes her look as "fairly conservative, within minimal variation in terms of skirt length (from just below knee to mid-calf), cut of the jacket, collar on the shirt, and color of the suit—generally navy, black, charcoal grey. "On occasion, I'll wear a lighter suit—provided that I don't have meetings with upper level management. If it's an upper level meeting, then I will definitely wear my darker suits."

Rose absolutely sees a correlation between dress and success. She patterns her own and her employees' behavior on the expected IBM style, taking the responsibility to advise those below her to dress the corporate part. "You're not only selling your information, you're selling yourself. How you appear is how you sell yourself."

*"You're not only
selling
information;
you're selling
yourself."*

"Plenty" is what Rose spends to maintain her corporate image, opting for high quality manufacturer suits like Kasper and Harvè Bernard, closed pumps and few, or often, no accessories. The corporate hierarchy of IBM is very defined and recognizable. In mergers, IBM carefully incorporates new acquisitions into their culture. Team players are rewarded and promoted.

"I know that when the big guys come to our location and I'm going to prepare a presentation for them, I'm going to wear my navy suit and white shirt. When I've done that, my manager has said that was the appropriate way."

Anybody who deals with clients should tailor her clothing to a client's particular tastes. At the same time, since your product is you, your clothes should manifest your personality or your skill (such as a great eye).

—Glamour

4

Category II: Communicator Dress

This category, *Communicator,* embraces companies involved in marketing and sales, manufacturing, real estate, education, and insurance. These companies are people oriented. They make connections, they serve and meet customer needs. Values prized in this category are charisma, accessibility, customer focus. In other words, the organizations in this category reward people who are creative problem-solvers, people who are capable of partnering and forming relationships with clients.

Cultural Values

These values are similar to Category I, but the companies which inhabit Category II are less formal. They are organized and practical, but with a certain amount of flair. The infrastructure, as with Category I, is in place, but more value is placed on spontaneity, change, and personality. The rhythm of this culture is more upbeat, more energetic, "more deadline driven." Walk through a Category II company and you will be aware of a lot more noise, a lot more people in bull sessions, and in general, a more flexible, relaxed atmosphere. Companies in this category include The Prudential, Trammel Crow, Century 21, Sears, the Dayton Hudson Department Stores Corporation, Galeries Lafayette.

Dress here is "dressed-down." It is a relaxed version of Category I. Here, individuals dress to make the other party feel comfortable. Category I clothing, which acts more like a symbol of security when their clients need them, is too high key, too formal, and can make the people you're dealing with uncomfortable when you're in a selling or problem-solving situation. Category II strikes a balance between competence and accessibility. Your dress assures your clients that you are competent, but does not create so much distance that they are unwilling to share concerns.

In Category II, then, there is a need to soften the guidelines outlined in Category I. This is effectively done largely through color and texture. For women, jackets and skirts need not be confined to solid colors; small plaids and tweeds are excellent choices, and by teaming solids with tweeds, for example, one "relaxes" the traditional uniform. Lighter colors like tan, camel, and khaki also have this affect. Black, which can be too formal for the *Communicator*, needs to be complemented with color, pattern, and jewelry so that it becomes a striking design background. There's a lot more leeway for blouses in Category II. Colors, understated stripes, prints, and geometric patterns work well here. Tailored dresses worn with a jacket carry out the less formal, more relaxed look of the *Communicator*. Accessories, too, can be more obvious in this category.

For men, the colors, shapes, and fabrics are similar to those in Category I. But in Category II, men can be more experimental with color. For example, they can select a suit which has an unusually bright thread in the fabric. You may, occasionally, see double-vented and double-breasted suits here. Shirts will be slightly more adventurous—obvious stripes, a subtle play of colors like pale peach, ecru, and gray. And stronger "statement" ties debut, ties that transcend the boundaries of Category I, but not so bold that they offend Category I sensibilities.

Organizations in this category are people-and product-oriented; they provide personal services. Functions which fit this category include:

- Sales
- Marketing
- Education
- Personnel
- Newly established, high growth industries

Because the emphasis here is on communication, the look of Category II is less formal, with more leeway in shape and color.

	Shape	*Color*	*Fabric*
Business Suits and Dresses	Practical More relaxed Semi-traditional suits and sports jackets	Mix of colors and patterns Stripes	Herringbone Tweed Silk Nailshead Flannel Linen Loose bulky weaves Knits
Blouses and Shirts	Same as I More refined shapes More detail	Same as I Strong colors Relaxed prints	Same as I

Overall, a good deal more variation is possible in *Communicator* dress than in *Corporate* dress. Thus, it's important to consider with whom you're dealing and what their conditioning toward clothes is likely to be. In selling insurance or real estate, for example, you want your clients to feel comfortable with you while still recognizing your competence and professionalism. Your goal is *to communicate both trust and credibility*. And, as with *Corporate* dress, quality is important—but the degree of expense must be carefully gauged to meet client's expectations. (The chart at the end of this chapter provides guidelines for Category II dressing.)

The individuals in this chapter represent a variety of Category II organizations. Each recognizes the importance of putting his or her clients at ease, of dressing with personal flair as well as meeting clients' expectations. But the thing you will notice is that there is no one "look." Yes, there's a certain degree of relaxation in the style, but there's a lot more variety — from the relaxed, playful dress of Meg Osman to the easy knit of Cynthia Mayeda to the Armani double-breasted suit of Mark Lamia who are profiled in the upcoming pages. Each sports a very distinctive look.

*Roxanne Givens
president*

Warm, relaxed, and supremely confident are adjectives which describe Roxanne Givens, *INC.* magazine's 1989 "Entrepreneur of the Year" for real estate development.

This confidence is carried through to Roxanne's style in dress. Although she confesses to be a reactionary—a Bohemian—her clothes reflect the classic, timeless qualities of good styling and attention to detail. "If everyone's wearing suits, I won't," she says. "Maybe that's the rebellious side of me. Now, when everyone's wearing dresses, I just might jump into a suit."

After work, however, she pulls out the stops. Her trademark, big, wild earrings, is toned down for business. Of her style she says, "I don't get hung up with fashion trends. My clothes could be in or out of style, so long as I feel good and make a good presentation."

Roxanne has forged a career out of the legacy her father left her. Less than two years after he founded Rainbow Development, a firm committed to providing housing for senior citizens, first time buyers, and low income people, he died, leaving the business to Roxanne. Roxanne had to learn the ropes while running the business, and today Rainbow Development boasts 1200 units in Minneapolis. "In 1990," Roxanne says, "we're taking the show on the road, expanding to other cities."

"My clothes can be in or out of style, so long as I feel good and make a good presentation."

This is not a paint by numbers game. Sometimes Roxanne feels that people's perceptions are that it should be, and that it probably is. "Even in the second generation, here at Rainbow," she says, "there's work ahead—even though some things were already underway."

"And here, as in any other business, respect doesn't come automatically with the territory. You have to earn it."

Roxanne is a spiritual person. She believes everything comes from God. "Once you have that," she affirms, "then, it's a sense of 'I can-ness.' Oh, there are roadblocks. . . . it seems that the road to success is always under construction."

This sense of 'I can-ness' is very strong in the way Roxanne runs her company. She believes in surrounding herself with people who know more than she in certain areas so that she can capitalize on their expertise. Perhaps this confidence in herself, as well as in others, is why the culture is slowly moving from authoritarian to participative. Roxanne says, "I used to be a dictator, and I have worked on that. I would prefer a team environment, but it doesn't happen over night. My employees know that my door is always open."

Rainbow Development will be changing its name to Legacy—and for Roxanne, that's significant because she is running the legacy her father left, a legacy she hopes to leave to her daughter one day.

Mark Lamia
director

"We sell jewelry, but we also sell ourselves," emphasizes Mark La-mia, a tall Texan of Italian heritage, who has travelled the world over. He is currently the Director of Precious Jewelry for Neiman-Marcus in Beverly Hills. The culture of this fine specialty store has been with Lamia his entire life. He describes his father, who worked for Neiman-Marcus for twenty-two years, as "The epitome of the well-dressed man anywhere in the world. He's sixty now, and he's still this incredibly handsome Italian, a veritable silver-haired devil. . . . actually a Neiman-Marcus legend. So you can see I've got pretty big shoes to fill. If I can accomplish one-tenth of what my father has, I'd be satisfied."

Lamia's fashion expertise has been cultivated since childhood when his parents dressed him and his brother as "dapper dudes." He found he liked the response of people to his good grooming. "People like to be complimented. I certainly use it in my selling. I find something I can honestly compliment—hair, clothes, perfume—without patronizing, and I make a point of commenting on it."

"I'd be a liar if I said I've never judged anyone on appearance, but I learned early on not to do it. In my first job, I had a customer come in with dirty boots and a sweatshirt. He ended up buying $28,000 in jewelry from me. That wouldn't have happened if I'd made a summary judgment about him." Mark says he goes more by what people say than how they dress. "Many of my customers shop in their casual or business clothes. I don't often see them in the store in their more formal evening clothes."

"We've got to look like our product."

The tendency toward casual shopping attire is a change Lamia has seen since his father's Neiman-Marcus days. "I used to get dressed up to go downtown to see my Daddy at the store. Shopping at Neiman-Marcus was an event!" The commitment to quality at Neiman-Marcus has remained consistent, as has the tradition of customer service. Lamia obviously operates in a very elite area of the store and makes sure his staff is always impeccably dressed. "We're selling $200,000 items. We've got to look like our product." To reinforce his image, Lamia buys "more than a dozen, but less than twenty" suits or sportcoats and slacks, ranging from $700-$1200, plus shirts, ties, casual clothes and Ferragamo shoes. At 6'5" and 220 lbs. Lamia finds clothes by Italian designers fit him well; most of his current wardrobe consists of Armani suits. "If I wore a size eleven shoe, and a 42 regular," he says, "I'd probably spend twice as much!"

Meg Osman
vice president

Meg Osman, who is Vice President of Magna Marketing Services, was the Director of Sales Promotion for Jaeger, a clothing manufacturer, at the time of this interview. Meg, who once thought Jaeger "too conservative" for her, discovered that Jaeger's timeless, classic quality could be adapted to her own style. "It can be as simple as rolling up my sleeves or putting up the collar. I can wear my own top with it, or a pin that I think is funky, or a scarf, or something to make it my own, yet the clothes really haven't changed."

Jaeger, one hundred-five years old and based in the United Kingdom, has always been committed to "magnificent natural fabrics, fine tailoring, and high quality." Like the company itself, Jaeger clothes offer fluid designs in the classic tradition. Meg calls the Jaeger look "investment dressing—tremendous quality that makes everybody feel good about owning it."

Meg has four considerations in choosing her clothing daily. First, she goes over her daily schedule. Is she travelling for location shots, meetings with clients — in house or public — going to a social event, etc.? "I check my schedule before I leave my office at night so I know what to lay out to wear the next day." Second, she selects what best expresses her individual style and mood, and makes sure she feels good in it. Third, she always wears Jaeger, and fourth, she finds out what the weather is doing today in New York.

For example, for a special luncheon for *Town & Country*, she combined classic Jaeger with her own touches for an overall soft, but really put-together look. She wore a light, "face-powder"-colored sweater with a white collar over a short black and white checked skirt ("I like short skirts"), heels, and minimal jewelry. "I felt entirely comfortable, absolutely me, yet very neat and thought out."

Jaeger tapped into Osman's fashion instincts to give them the pulse of what's going on in the stores, especially in North America. "We need to tweak the clothing and the promotion for the American market." She describes the company as "a warm family, headed by our lovely, impeccable president Rodney Johnson." She describes Jaeger as a place that fosters "open communication and supportive work relationships grounded on a tradition of excellence."

Now, in her new position at Magna Marketing (among their clients, Ralph Lauren and the American Cotton Council), Meg is as at home in short skirts, dark hosiery, and boots when she's out on a photo shoot as she is in a suit for a client meeting.

Jimmy Lawrence
president

Jimmy Lawrence has created an amalgamation in his company, Lawrence Associates. His background is varied; he was a stockbroker and financial consultant. He has studied interior design, carpentry, and architecture, and this background forms the basis of the synergistic business he runs today. Lawrence Associates does demographic consulting with large companies to relocate their transferred executives to either an existing house or a custom-built home. Although it sounds quite far ranging, his business is really very focused. Lawrence and his partner have designed an atmosphere that "encourages creativity under the umbrella of a functioning, acceptable corporate structure. We don't have a lot of rules, but we stress competence and graciousness."

This air of gracious competence carries Lawrence into any locale. His personal clothing style is understated, high quality garments, (usually gabardines) in a wide range of colors. "My favorite color combination is navy, tan, and burgundy. I can give you any look with some basic pieces." His after-hour style is "totally eclectic. I wear anything. I like jeans, shorts, silk suits, tuxedos. It depends on where I'm going." Lawrence chooses elegantly classic pieces that will "stand the test of time. I listen to what's happening in fashion, but I don't let anyone tell me what I should or shouldn't wear. I'm not trendy."

Lawrence consciously tailors his choice of attire for his clients. "If I'm seeing a more conservative businessman, I'll dress in deference to his comfort. But I'm always me. The quality of my work speaks for itself, not my trying to be somebody." An aura of confidence emanates from Lawrence and he feels this puts people at ease. "I believe you should be as comfortable talking to a CEO as a streetperson because the only difference between them is some arbitrary, external definition of success."

His egalitarian approach infuses his workplace, which has a intimate "we're-all-in-this-together" attitude. " We don't allow ourselves to take each other too seriously. You've got to maintain a sense of perspective about what's really important. Business is a game. About once or twice a week, my partner (a woman) and I get together, wink, and say, "Is this fun or what?!" He's of the opinion that too much structure inhibits creativity.

". . . I don't let anyone tell me what I should or shouldn't wear."

Jan Schonwetter
president

"I see clothes as a definition of who I am." For Jan Schonwetter, owner and President of the twenty-five year old franchise of Mid-west Weight Watchers, this relatively simple statement sums up a complex evolutionary process. It's one she's been working through for years, and many of us never reach. "I used to buy in stages. I had the idea that I needed different clothes for each thing I did, each role I was playing. Now what I'm doing is combining the whole idea, figuring I'm me no matter where I am. A style that is appropriate for me, for anywhere I go." The key to her personal style is "Simplifying—learning who I am and being true to it."

The path which Jan has taken to arrive at this point in her personal expression is closely related to her professional experience with Weight Watchers. Jan found that as her sense of self worth changed, so too did her style of dress. "When I was very fat, I didn't want people to notice me, so I dressed to hide. After I lost weight, I wanted to be noticed, so I dressed in bright colors. Now I'm in a period where I just want to be comfortable and really look the best I can."

"I see clothes as a definition of who I am."

Jan has found that clothing is no longer a protection or a definition of who she is. "As I become more comfortable with me, I am more comfortable in my clothes, and the more comfortable I am in my environment. It's like this little ripple that starts out and goes further and further and further, a ripple of comfort and ease in myself and my clothing."

This process of self-growth is the crux of Jan's business philosophy. "The image of Weight Watchers is really to help men, women, and children find that part of themselves they want to treat with kindness, gentleness, and approval. Then they can do the things that will be right for them." With her employees, she continues to build on their feelings of self worth. "I am a team builder, an integrator. I believe in giving people a chance to fulfill their own destiny. It's much more feminine. Instead of being authoritarian, I formed a team." Part of that confidence building is done through seminars with fashion consultants which she offers to her staff two to four times a year.

Jan Schonwetter acknowledges the impact women role models in Weight Watchers have made on her and sees herself as a role model for her own staff and clients. "I cannot stress how important role models are for the evolving person. We may not say, 'Gee, I want to look like you,' but we see something in them that stands out, and we think, 'That's the way I want to be.'"

Cynthia Mayeda
managing director

Cynthia Mayeda, managing director of the Dayton Hudson Foundation, oversees the corporate giving program of Minnesota's largest retail chain. And like its parent corporation, the foundation is very much service-driven and very much a part of the community. "Our giving philosophy," Cynthia says, "has changed little from its beginning. We've had a long time to learn about the focus—about the areas in which we give—so that we've had the opportunity to become experts. We subscribe to the idea of community service, and our contributions impact the quality of life in the thirty-seven states the Dayton-Hudson Department Stores are located."

Of her own operation, Cynthia says, "We're the Harlem Globe Trotters. We work as a team. All of us understand the values, communication is open, and esprit is really strong. Because of the work we do, we need to self disclose — to talk about what we think, how we feel our performance is relative to the community's performance. As a result, we probably know a lot more about each other's emotional and personal life, and this is a critical factor which creates this incredible team work."

This openness, this willingness to be vulnerable, is very much a part of Cynthia's style. She puts a high premium on curiosity, problem solving, and hard work.

Although Cynthia meets a lot of different people in the not-for-profit sector, she doesn't dress differently. She says, "I dress for me, much more so than anybody else. That's why dress codes never affect me very much." Her approach to dress may be characterized as eclectic. She wears a lot of knits, a lot of black. Some days, she's more formal, other days less so. She moves easily between knits and unstructured Asian designs.

"People who are smart and aware will figure out what's appropriate. . . . It won't be the first thing they think about, but it will be part of their thinking."

Prior to moving to the Foundation, Cynthia was managing director of the Cricket Theatre. When she made the move from the arts to big business, she promised herself she would never buy a navy suit, and although suits have been redefined, she doesn't wear them. "I never liked the idea behind the suit; it never appealed to me because I'm not a tailored person." Now that dresses have become acceptable in the work place, have become a substitute for the "uniform," she says she feels like a reactionary. "I started wearing more two pieces. I think I dress exactly the opposite of what's 'in'."

The whole idea of invisibility, of not wearing clothes that say something about you is anathema to Cynthia. "Dress," she says, "should be exactly the opposite."

Like Roxanne Givens, Cynthia is "mad" for earrings and shoes. Her dress choices tend to be knits by Helen Hsu and the comfortable, architectural designs of Californian Sue Wong.

Supremely happy, Cynthia says "You won't meet anyone else, no matter how many interviews you conduct, who loves his or her work more than I do."

5

Category III:
Creative Dress

Creative—the third category—covers the more creative industries—advertising, public relations, interior design, retailing, the arts, and certain entrepreneurial ventures.

Cultural Norms

Here, the cultural norm is more free-wheeling, more expressive, more innovative. The emphasis is on personal freedom and individuality. In this culture, imagination and creativity are the buzz words. Because the companies in this category have so much to do with design, people outside these fields have certain expectations. They expect that the people who will be designing their offices, their advertising, and so on, will be imaginatively dressed, will have a certain aesthetic appreciation for line and color, for shape and texture, and that they will put themselves together in a statement-making way. How one puts oneself together, then, is often a measure of how creative and innovative he or she will be in working with the client.

It should be noted, however, that if creative dress is too "extreme," it sends up a red flag to clients. I know of at least two interior designers who lost major contracts because their "creative" dress looked messy to the client. The banker client of one said, "I couldn't have my bank look like that!"

Category III dressing is creative—but it still reads "business." It means being able to combine the right pieces with the appropriate degree of *panache*. It's also the hardest look to describe. As one of the Supreme Court Justices remarked about pornography—"I can't tell you what it is, but I know it when I see it."

The following chart illustrates some key elements that distinguish the *Creative* look.

Category III: Creative

As the name suggests, this category is represented by people in creative fields:

- Interior design
- Retail, especially boutiques
- Advertising
- Commercial Art
- Entrepreneurial companies

This category has the greatest latitude since it generally uses clothes as a means of expression—clothing more as an art form (which, in fact, is a form of uniform.)

	Shape	Color	Fabric
Business Suits and Dresses	Line and design an influential factor	Taupe	Same as I and II
		Peach	Loose weaves
	Loose fitting, very relaxed with or without ties	Bronze Basics	
Blouses and Shirts	Same as I and II Unusual design More relaxed Elongated line Exaggerated design	Striking color	Same as I and II

Men in Category III respond to Euro-designed suits: shaped jackets, double-breasted, and fitted at the waist. They wear more color: mauve, taupe, bronze, and plum; and also plaids and patterns with Chinese red and blue accents. Shirts, generally tapered, are in peach, mauve, pewter, and off-white. Ties reek creativity—the colors are mixed and brighter; the designs are bolder. In some cultures, men in Category III wear suits with no tie at all. The men in this category also wear tie shoes, but they are designed by Italian or French craftsmen. And when they wear slip-ons, they're likely to be exquisitely crafted by French or Italian shoemakers.

Women in this category wear less structured suits, suits where the shape is defined by the body it covers. You'll find more coordinated separates which can be interchanged, yet bear the mark of individuality, to reflect one's personal style. Dresses, too, are a staple in the *Creative* closet—tents, knits with raglan sleeves, often belted with an expensive leather belt and antique buckle.

Generally speaking, you're more likely to see in this Category contemporary designs, trendy looks, and bolder colors—clothes which are chosen for art, for design.

The men and women featured in this chapter dress as diversely as any Category III people world-wide. Each combines personal flair and a distinctive look appropriate for the culture in which they operate. Representatives of Category III range broadly from the more formal dressing of individuals at a magazine like *Town & Country*, to the casual elegance of Martine Bercu, to the continental style of Bob Dillon.

Fred Jackson, III
publisher

As publisher of the elite *Town & Country* magazine, Fred Jackson, III, is both a fashion follower and a fashion pacesetter. Savvy people look to him and his publication to see how the other half lives. "I work for *Town & Country* twenty-four hours a day, whether at the supermarket, a polo match, traveling on an airplane, or at the office. I *am* Town & Country, just as everyone who works here is. What I do, how I do it, what I say and how I address people—there's an impression left there."

Jackson recognizes the importance of good presentation. He knows that consciously or unconsciously people judge your company through its people. How they appear may determine someone's business choices. His own style was influenced by his father. "My father's group was influenced by Adolphe Menjou, the Duke of

Windsor, and Douglas Fairbanks." Today, he laments, there are no such sartorial models.

In order to get ahead, he recommends that individuals really make themselves aware of their environment. "Be concerned with those around you. Who's immediately ahead of you—how they conduct themselves in meetings or on the phone. Watch their demeanor . . . how they treat others . . . how they dress . . . and emulate the characteristics that will help you succeed."

Jackson points out that America doesn't have a rigid class system based on accent such as exists in England, but "there are truly so many giveaways. The whole thing has to do with being accepted, being viewed as part of the team. Dress is clearly the most important thing. It's the first message you send."

The *Town & Country* staff sports a range of fashion choices from traditional Brooks Brothers suits to the most current designer looks. But there is always a polished, sophisticated, cultivated persona. "You can't wear white socks and work for *Town & Country*." If Jackson has an employee he thinks has the potential to succeed in the charged world of top magazine publishing but hasn't quite got "the look," he won't hesitate to take that person aside and give him or her advice on style. He has even gone so far as to take them shopping and to send them to classes in deportment. "You never hear someone say 'I'm from *Town & Country*, only to have the other party say, 'No, you're not.'" At *Town & Country*, we cultivate the clothes, the speech, the style . . . the whole package."

"You only launch once."

Martine Bercu
president

    "I project the European look. When people see me, they think I've bought my clothes abroad, but I don't. I just know how to put it together." Roche-Bobois, a French-based furniture company, is the setting for chic Martine Bercu, president of the Minneapolis franchise. She characterizes the European flair as "a difference in my process of thinking. The whole American population is either extremely casual or extremely dressed up. My look is a combination of casual and dressy."

    Whereas an American would buy an "outfit" which goes together perfectly, Europeans would use a blend of color and fabric to create something slightly unexpected, a sense of "subtle anarchy." The key is keeping an up-to-date look through accessories—colors, accents, and trendy touches. Fashion trends strongly influence French choices. "They adopt it, wear it, and then it's gone. Clothes have to be updated all the time."

A put-together French look probably consists of several tops, expensive sweaters—and a few skirts and pants. These pieces, in solid colors, can be intermixed in a variety of options. An example would be to combine a short leather skirt, an expensive sweater, and a khaki jacket, with some good, but not ostentatious jewelry—maybe a very good watch. "You must isolate the pieces and use your imagination."

Martine sees the French using clothing as a definition of status. "They spend money on their clothes and it shows right away. In America, there are other standards for status and the clothes might not show it." Yet Europeans don't go for the ostentatious—big diamonds and lots of gold. "Never like 'Dynasty' or 'Dallas.' It's very rare for the French to be overdressed."

". . . isolate the pieces and use your imagination."

Bob Dillon
president

"The worst thing I can be is not color coordinated." So says Bob Dillon, entrepreneurial wizard behind Colorcurve color communications systems, who admits he's a clothes hound, "but not to the point of being ridiculous about it." Dillon sees clothing as a part of the business package as well as an extension of personality, intelligence, and integrity. People who aren't put together maybe don't get that first chance."

In his business, Dillon must appeal to a broad spectrum of people from flashy New York designers, to chemical engineers in lab coats, to corporate CEOs. "I dress for occasions, and I like to have fun with color. I buy typically conservative clothes, but I have some latitude because of my business." Within his basically conservative style, he accessorizes with colorful ties, handkerchiefs, and socks. "It would be terrible if I walked in [to a meeting with a client] and I was just this mundane, non-color individual."

Dillon's work takes him from Los Angeles to Iowa, New York, Paris, and Milan. On the international vista, he distinguishes specific differences between American and European fashion. "Europeans spend a lot of money on few [pieces of] clothing, whereas Americans (being a more disposable society), buy more. A European would buy one or two great suits for the season and wear them over and over, until they're worn out. The Europeans are a little more daring and less programmed. They have that innate ability to put things together and carry it off. I have clothing that I buy there and wear specifically for Europe so I don't look too American."

"I dress for occasions."

If Europe remains the international leader in style, Dillon sees Americans taking a big lead in the realm of color. "Right now the fashion statement in Europe is three things: black, black, or black. But color is a major factor in whether a product sells or doesn't. So today, the top designers in Paris are using incredible primary colors. It's very American and they love it because it's broken them out of that black-on-black syndrome."

Jim Binger
owner

Former president of Honeywell, Jim Binger is currently the owner of Jujamcyn, a string of five Broadway theatres. A go-getter, Binger's style is pretty fluid, both in dress and management style. In the days when Binger was with Honeywell it was a company on the move. The atmosphere was "pretty casual. My door was always open. We tried to generate a relaxed feeling, almost giving the impression of being disorganized to promote the energy essential in R & D."

Honeywell was generally a shirt-sleeve organization. Binger has observed there are different styles between corporations. "If I went to see people in IBM, they had their jackets on. If I went to General Electric, they often did not. You know — it's sort of a signature of the organization." Within Honeywell, he also identifies informal dress codes. "The marketing department was the better dressed.

They wore jackets and ties. The engineers would wear ties, their shirt-sleeves rolled up. The salesmen out in the field would modify their dress depending on the client."

Binger would like to believe appearance doesn't determine ability, but acknowledges there is some correlation—albeit subconscious—between external deportment and an impression of competence. "Someone may not look correct, but they're smart and productive. It doesn't necessarily mean they are going to function differently or they don't understand the rules." In spite of his belief, he finds himself prey to the first impression syndrome. "I was talking to an artistic director from a local theatre. The guy looks terrible. It's taken me two years to understand he was a lot better than he looked." He doubts he would ever send this particular person to meet potential backers. "Not everyone will meet with him as frequently as I have to find out how good he is. I think the initial reaction would be, 'What are you giving me here?'"

*Julie Pinkwater
vice president*

Julie Pinkwater, senior Vice President and Director of Media Planning for McCaffrey and McCall, Inc., takes her job very seriously, but likes to have fun while doing it. "I'm allowed to be creative. Advertising operates on a very high energy level. Things are constantly happening. Media changes every day. Our clients change every day. It's really a balancing act."

In order to operate in this fast paced, fluid environment, McCaffrey and McCall have created an "open door" workplace. "We work in teams. Junior and senior account executives, media personnel, creative people. It's very open. We have a lot of channels to go through, but hopefully they're growth channels." She sees the open door as very symbolic of the entire climate of McCaffrey and McCall. "We all answer our own phones around here. . . . that's [the cue] from David McCall. It's a culture which transcends all levels. Accessibility is very important."

Reflective of this company, dress is also flexible. "No one dictates demeanor. There is no uniform here." Style choices vary between groups, and certain subtle tendencies can be identified. The account executives tend toward the conservative side—Paul Stuart and Brooks Brothers suits, Gucci loafers, button-down shirts. The creative people are generally a little softer, a little more chic. Among media, the look is not structured, but always "put together." Julie, one of few women at this level, selects classic looks with designer overtones. She prefers suits to dresses ("I've never seen a dress that knocked me over") and feels perfectly comfortable dressed in slacks. "But there are certain clients with whom I wouldn't wear pants." In general, Julie feels, "Europeans aren't very comfortable with businesswomen in pants."

Frequent trips to Germany, (her parents were born in Europe,) give Julie intimate experience with European tastes. "Europeans have much more style than Americans. They accept certain kinds of dress more easily, so I dress as fashionably as I can without being avant garde." In her role as media director, Julie minimally accommodates her look for the client's expectations and comfort. "When you're dressed casually, I think people perceive you'll be more casual. I handle my choices according to who I'll be seeing."

"Advertising is a visual business. Appearance is important. . . . To a certain degree, it's an indication of talent. If someone is a 'turn off', they have to work harder to convince you of their talent."

David Gahr

Rick Dobbis
executive vice
president

"RCA is a creative company in a creative business. We demand that people here stretch themselves," declares Rick Dobbis, Executive Vice President of RCA records. Based in New York, Dobbis heads a group of dynamic thinkers who have completely changed the entire culture of the RCA label in the past two and a half years.

With his keen eye for packaging, Dobbis points out that individuality of expression is crucial for the fresh approach in his company. "The basic environment is wide open. A lot of kibitzing. A lot of 'wait a minute. . . . wait a minute, I think this!' It's very volatile and action-oriented. That's why most of us are here. We love the music and we love the excitement."

Returning to the former image of the pioneer RCA, the company has brought back the original lightning bolt logo. "It fits. It fits the personality of where our company is going today."

Walking through Dobbis's offices, you see a wide spectrum of styles, with people wearing sports clothes to jeans. "Dress is a product of individual expression. Our rules are much different in the arts." But even in the arts Dobbis notes there is a kind of "casual uniform," especially in film. "In our company . . . and this is something I'm happy about . . . you will see the full range. Executives in jeans and junior people in suits. There's absolutely no code at all. It's really a matter of personal style and expression."

Dobbis chooses his daily wardrobe on the basis of agenda and mood. "Normally the more I have to get 'up' for the day, the more dressed I'll get. I use dress as a personal uniform. On Fridays, I'm usually in jeans." A man who is attuned to visual clues, Dobbis recognizes the psychological impact his clothes can make. "I might dress with the grain or against the grain, depending on what it is that I'm trying to achieve." His signature is pins—lapel pins, collar pins, tie pins. "I like to dress so it satisfies me. There's something individual about the way I put things together."

"Dress is a product of individual expression within the context of the music industry . . . and there's a wider range of choices possible."

Summary

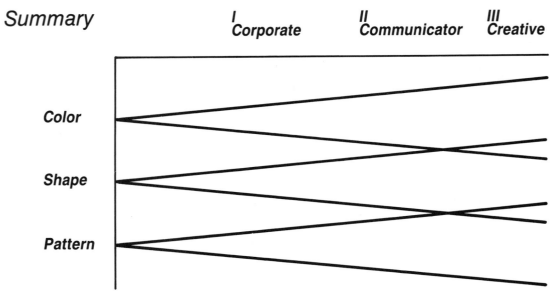

As you move from Category I to Category III, color, shape, and pattern become more relaxed and less formal. The move from I to III means a greater degree of freedom, a greater latitude to accent your personal style—to choose clothes that are less restrictive, less predictable.

6

Global People:
The Cognoscenti

Dior. Givenchy. Chanel. Balenciaga. Pierre Cardin.

Designer names which dominated the fashion industry from World War II through the Sixties. Names which your grandmothers and mothers knew well. Names which stood for chic, for haute couture, whose influence in women's clothing dictated what most women—not merely the wealthy and the famous—looked like for decades.

The phenomenon of the French influence, especially in America, is certainly not new. As a new nation—a nation of upstarts—we wanted so very much to be thought sophisticated, cultured, even continental. So we adopted and imported from abroad—especially from England and France—furniture, fabric, clothing, art, theatre, everything that was not indigenous to America.

Los Angeles. London. Paris. Tokyo. New York.
Milan. Madrid.

Cities which now dominate the fashion scene. Yes, there are the Chanels, the House of Dior, and the St. Laurents. But what has happened to the fashion industry in recent years is its internationalization. It is what designer Jean-Paul Gaultier calls *metissage*—a cultural and historical cross-breeding. No longer do the French or the English or the Americans dominate how the world dresses. What has happened with global travel, global business, and accelerated international competition is the increased influx of trends and ideas from other countries.

Who can forget, in the late Sixties, the wonderfully romantic clothing that flooded American stores after "Dr. Zhivago"? Or the long, flowing burnoose in subtle desert colors which appeared in the stores during the Oil Crisis, when Arabs seemed to be buying up America?

This *metissage* is more than a trend. As countries wax and wane in influence, so too does their impact on the more mundane aspects of an international economy. Over the last 12 years, the influences and trends that have invaded the marketplace are as much an acknowledgement of who's in power, or who's on the way up, as they are to what is merely fashionable.

It is the visual expression of an international cultural synthesis trend watchers say has been long in the making. Herman Kahn, writer and futurologist, writing in the Seventies, argued that with the spread of the Beatles' influence, pop culture became internationalized. "Perhaps in 1985, an Italian, Tanzanian, Bolivian or Turk will listen to an Icelandic pop singer on a Thai-made transistor radio, wearing clothes designed in a boutique in Seoul," Kahn predicted. Today, information travels with a speed even Kahn might not have anticipated.

Pop culture and fashion transcend national boundaries to reflect the kind of world we live in today, a world which is largely open door, one country to the next, where what's "in" is communicated via the media as soon as someone notices it's "in"; a world where a name is not as important as a feeling, an ambiance, or a look.

A walk down the street of any major city in the world will illustrate what has happened to fashion here, and more particularly, abroad.

Extravagant dress is the dandy's signature.

Beau Brummel . . . felt at least the equal of anyone he ever met. Brummel's amazing appearance blotted out his lack of a title. In a world where, after the French Revolution, fashion had fallen out of favor and style had troughed, he triumphed. During the revolutionary years, clothes themselves had been revolutionized. In England, the result was an abandonment of formality. Not until Brummel shook fashion by the coattails did the English have a right to be called elegant again.
—Patrick Kinmonth, "fine and dandy," *Vogue*

Neighbor Close

As the world shrinks, as men and women interact across borders and penetrate countries, the need to know cultural dress symbols becomes even more important. Like a foreign language, the language of dress and its system of signs needs to be learned if one is to operate successfully in a world which has become increasingly international, a veritable polyglot of nations. Knowing a foreign language, knowing the dress language of a particular culture or country gives one an individual freedom. Just as you learn the language of a country so you can say exactly what you mean, learning the dress language of the countries you work in (and incorporating culturally accepted symbols into your own dress) enables you to successfully do what you need to do. You can blend in. You can easily operate — whether negotiating a merger, making a big sale, or lobbying for relief in trade tariffs.

As more and more people move to other countries as fluidly as they used to move to other cities, as more and more companies begin to do business abroad, as more social and political barriers are removed between nations, daily global travel becomes an integral part of business life. You can see, then, how important it is to know the language of the country to which you're traveling and how important it is to be in tune with cultural mores, prohibitions, and taboos so that you and your clothes do not offend, do not get in the way of doing business. Even much-traveled royalty can run into problems over questions of protocol and tradition.

On a recent visit to a Near Eastern country, England's Princess Diana wore the appropriate dress, modest in color, shape, and design. Everything was going well until she crossed her legs, exposing them, and thereby offending her Arab host. If it can happen to royalty who employ experts in protocol, dress, and mores, think how much more vulnerable you can be.

Before you go abroad, find out as much as you can about the country to which you're traveling: its hallmarks of style, its cultural dress norms at the host company, its predominant symbols, and its weather at that particular time of year. Regardless of where you're going, there are some guidelines that you can follow to adapt your basic wardrobe so that you effectively blend in with the culture of

Clothing statements vary from country to country. It's a wise traveler who knows what to say.
—Susan Smith, *Men's Fashions of the Times*

When traveling, your priorities have to change. In your own country, you have the luxury of indulging your esthetic. Abroad, you have to consider propriety — you are, after all, a guest.
—Richard Merkin, *Men's Fashions of the Times*

the country, thus putting your hosts at ease and therefore, confident of your competence and credibility.

International Know-how

Evidence of the pervasiveness of this integration of cultures shows up most often in what the *New York Times* calls the "style-conscious young" who are in the know about "what's hip, what's hot or current on the street. They have forged a vocabulary that might include such oddly assorted elements as a fringed American cowboy jacket, German track shoes, a Soviet Army trench coat, a kilim-patterned vest, or dainty Edwardian knickers picked up at a London flea market." However it shows up, the young are unerringly more global. For example, the Russian glasnost was accompanied by the emergence of "rock" dress—jeans and sweatshirts with sayings on them or with symbols of rock groups, and with Adidas or Reeboks.

This cultural melange or *metissage* mirrored in the clothes of the world's young today has been going on since the dawn of civilization. After the Romans conquered Britain, togas were the standard dress of the prosperous; when the Normans invaded England in 1066, French styles were the new measure of chic. The Crusaders brought exotic styles back from the Holy Land—Saracen turbans, Turkish pointed shoes, and Jewish steeple headdresses—and new, exotic colors like azure and lilac. The Japanese emergence as an international power in the nineteenth century saw the introduction of Japanese prints, fans, pottery, and clothes. Fur coats became fashionable at the turn of the century in Paris, London, and New York after the alliance of France and Russia in the 1890s and 1900s.

Today, you can look in any European or American fashion magazine, and you can immediately spot European models wearing clothes from European designers or Americans in Euro designs. There's a distinctive look—a trigger that signals "foreign," as well as details which blend with our own culture. So too, individuals around the world have that "look," that same dynamic.

Yes, dress is truly a cultural phenomenon. Just as we have adopted, adapted, and imitated through the centuries, it becomes imperative today for the international traveler to adapt, and, to a certain extent, follow dress norms valued in each country as well.

After the Thirty Years' War, around the l650's, the ladies of Dusseldorf inaugurated the *decolleté*, uncovering lots of bosom, sprinkled with lace and flowers, generally in pastel colors. . . .
—*International Herald Tribune*

On certain levels, of course, the world expects Americans to be Americans, Frenchmen to be Frenchmen, and so on. But they also respect and admire those who become acculturated, those who are sensitive enough to soften up, for example, a blatantly American look. This sensitivity speeds up communication and acceptance. There is a certain polish that shows up in truly international business people. They have a special ease and a familiarity with foreign dress accents which please—a blending of cultures that is indefinable. Often the blend is a wonderful mix; for example, a Savile Row suit, an Italian tie, French shoes, and an American shirt.

The same sentiment is reciprocal when a European or other foreign national acknowledges our style by adapting some of our idiosyncracies. Many a Japanese returns to his homeland sporting a cowboy hat, and distinctly American food shows up on his dinner table. This imitation is similar to our own frontier days when we adopted French interior design flair in homes, cuisine, behavior, and perfume as a sign of our admiration. China, too, is not only picking up Western clothing, but to some extent Western ideas of democracy (even considering the spring 1989 tragedy of Tiananmen Square. In fact, one of the reasons for that irrational tragedy could easily have been the nervousness of Chinese leaders who were reacting to the demands for democratic change in a culture that was already moving too quickly).

Cultural Gaffes

Just as dress works for or against you in your own city, company, and country, it can, on an international level, cause a personal affront. Dress can and does get in the way of doing business, especially when it distracts from a meeting's purpose. Several years ago, a young French businesswoman was attending a high level business meeting for her company in Los Angeles during one of the city's hottest summers. She arrived at the meeting impeccably dressed in crisp white linen *sans* hose. Her American colleagues found it difficult to do business—going "without hose" is just not something one does—even in freewheeling LA.

No one is immune to this kind of situation. President Reagan made international headlines by showing up for a meeting at Versailles in a green plaid suit. Nancy Reagan offended French

An associate in Cologne may not know about your charitable contributions or the daughter who graduated summa cum laude, but he will most readily see the cut of your jacket and the quality of your shirt.
—Richard Merkin, *Men's Fashions of the Times*

Richard Verin spent years in the European financial community and thought he knew about that impregnable bastion of sartorial *Diktat*, London's center of banking and finance, the City. On a

trip home to the United States Verin bought himself a gray suit with a Pierre Cardin label — not the regulation pinstripe but the faintest of checks, with a hint of a tapered cut. He was a smash in Chicago and a rave in New York. But when he marched into his office in the City. . . the reaction was withering. "Oh," said a colleague "Going out to the country for the weekend, are we?"
— *The World*

sensibilities by appearing at a fancy dress event in knickers. Raisa Gorbachev, wife of the Soviet President, wore rhinestone-decorated shoes during a daytime event in America and caused the press to make disparaging remarks about her selection.

In each of these instances, dress got in the way — dress became the focus of an event rather than the event itself. And in a world where efficiency and productivity are prized, letting your clothing get in the way of doing business is just not good business sense.

International Accents

Perhaps the best way to talk about the cultural differentiation between nations and to gain some sense of what is acceptable is to look at the way natives of one country see themselves, as well as the way they are different from other nationalities. Most of the people we interviewed for this section of the book were very candid with comments about their own people, as well as those from other countries. And, almost to a person, the most outstanding and differentiating feature discussed was hair.

For whatever reason, most Europeans, both male and female, seem to have less controlled hair (by control they mean a hairdresser look). Additionally, most Europeans (and of course, there are always going to be exceptions to the rule) are recognizable by their natural hair styles. (Very curly hair, on the one hand, seems to be distinctly American, and on the other hand, a signature of the Italian male.) Along with the straightness of the hair seems to go a less stylized, almost casual look. Unlike their American counterparts, European women don't look as though they just stepped out of the beauty salon. Their hair seems to flow; and its basic disarray is a creative one.

Men, too, have a less "controlled" hair style. Their hair is swept off the forehead, close to the sides, neatly trimmed in back, or loosely tumbling, on their foreheads. Germans and Englishmen tend to have much shorter hair than their Italian and French confreres. In fact, Alison Lurie in *The Language of Clothes*, contends that in England "a gentleman practically never wears sideburns or a hairstyle that covers his ears . . . ; if he has a mustache it must be of moderate size."

Another distinguishing characteristic or symbol of European women is their spare use of makeup. To most Europeans, American women look overly made up, especially by day — too much lipstick, heavy eyeshadow, and blusher. European women, on the other hand, look much less planned and thought out; naturalness seems to be much more prized than in America. In fact, in other countries, makeup is usually reserved for special events and for evenings. Martine Bercu, President of Roche-Bobois in Minneapolis, says that she hardly thinks about makeup once she has put it on in the morning. She says that American women seem to be preoccupied with makeup to the extent that they will repair their makeup during a meal in a restaurant. She sees this preoccupation, too, in hair styles and in fingernails. American women seem overly concerned with nails — nails that are longer than you will see on European women — nails which are, or seemingly are, manicured daily.

European men also notice this about American women and find it off putting. How can a woman be serious about business, they question, if she spends so much time worrying about her hair and her nails? (It's not that she does, of course, but the perception is that she does. On the other hand, Americans find a lack of respect for what they see as very casual grooming among most Europeans. And on our side, we must recognize that this penchant for "neatness" is very American.)

These are some of the small, but telling, details that distinguish Americans from Europeans — women more especially than men. But there are differences in European males, too. Earlier in the book, John Jay, creative director at Bloomingdale's, said that American men are too "packaged," too somber. They don't dress playfully — don't do the outrageous. While this might be true to some extent, there are some similarities between the male uniform in America and the male uniform in Europe. And while there are similarities, it does differ from country to country. Let's look at this in a little more detail.

The well-turned-out English businessman, for example, generally wears striped shirts, sometimes with contrasting collars, with just the right amount of cuff showing. Collars must be just so: not too long, not too pointed, not too round, and *never* button-down. Dark pin-striped suits are customarily from a Savile Row tailor, the trousers

Women [in America] for instance use much more color on the face, while Europeans prefer a natural look with the emphasis on a well-cared for complexion. The French idiosyncrasy — matte foundation/powder, bright red lipstick — is another Francophile influence.
— Beatrice Dautresme, L'Oreal, quoted in *Bazaar*

To the British, clothes add up to a complicated language of power, rich in accents, class distinctions and potential *faux*

pas — and heaven help the unsuspecting executive who misreads the cut of a suit or the length of a cuff.
— *The World*

cut fairly high in the waist with buttons to attach braces — and the braces* may be a shocking surprise of color or pattern. Belts are not generally worn, except on weekends and in the country. (It's important for Americans to recognize that the wide chalk stripe suit worn by the most eminent of City gents is not a reincarnation of Al Capone, who dressed in the European style in his heyday.)

The English are quite exacting in what constitutes a gentleman's wardrobe. Since the days of Beau Brummel, they have set the standard for the world for male dress.

French businessmen, too, wear a standard type of dress — closer fitting Euro-styled suits in dark, dusky, or subtle patterns, white shirts, colored and striped shirts, somber ties, and tie shoes in dark colors. When they wear pattern, their trousers and jackets do not match completely; rather, they are complementary. This constitutes their suit look. This look is not to be confused with the blazer and slacks combination espoused in America. What might be considered a way of dressing that is anathema in America is commonplace in France: light color socks worn to match shirts. Jean-Pierre Penhoat, a Frenchman working here in America, says that a Frenchman's choice of socks often reflects his individuality and oftentimes signals his playfulness.

It is only when you move to Italy that you see flamboyance and flair and individuality at its finest with all the finishing touches. The Italian feel for style invades the business world as much as it does the creative world.

In fact, many see Italians as the best dressed men in the world. " . . . they may embrace the best of English dress, but they have their own inimitable style. Certainly, the golden men sauntering down Milan's Via della Spiga in dove-gray wool and silk, or ecru linen wrinkled to perfection, a jacket tossed over one shoulder, a hand dug deep in a pocket, emanate an exhilarating glamour." (*Men's Fashions of the Times*)

---

* Americans call them suspenders. There is, however, a distinction. Braces button onto pants; suspenders clip on.

People and country watchers attribute this sense of style—which pervades every part of Italian life—to the Italian cultural heritage. Fred Jackson, publisher of *Town & Country* who travels extensively, sees the Italian style as "part and parcel of their lives." Everything is done with a certain exuberance, a certain energy. Italian men are sleek—their suits shaped, the look finished. And possibly more than any other men, they experiment more with fabric. They're not afraid to look rumpled in a wonderfully cut linen suit because that's how linen is supposed to look! They seem to be on stage, and the play is the thing.

While German professionals invest in their clothes, they, like their French and English counterparts, look alike. In fact, says Jackson, they all look like bankers. The Germans see clothing as functional, practical, and sturdy. Again, there is a certain discipline in dressing well.

The Japanese, like the Americans of old, emulated Western tradition. Hence, they tend to wear gray and navy suits and white shirts. Recently, however, there has been a trend toward a more Japanese look, as native designers look to their own culture for inspiration. This has meant an emphasis on comfort and textiles with unusual textures, and this loosening and softening is impacting the Western male market.

Women in France and Italy approach dress quite unlike the men in their countries. And one finds a discernible difference between the two countries. Both know how to put clothes together, know how to choose from an assortment of accessories and basics to create a look that is distinctly individual—a distinctively unique work of art. Part of this ability comes from their upbringing. Most French and Italian children are dressed like little adults. Clothes are a part of their lives from early on—there's little distinction between what are children's clothes and adult apparel. In these countries, children learn early to button a lot of buttons, to wear ties, to put on blouses which mirror the looks of their parents. Yes, their sense of style is inherent from birth. And dressing up belongs naturally in their lives for Sunday and ceremonial days. Americans, on the other hand, seem uncomfortable (especially young boys) in dress clothes.

Another factor in this unerring sense of style is that the latest look is readily available as soon as someone dictates it's "in." The shops

As far as men's fashion is concerned, the world is becoming more Italian all the time. The instinctive Italian approach to clothes . . . us[ing] a jacket, and most often, a tailored one, as the basis of dressing for almost any occasion or effect, be it businesslike, sporty, or rakish. And it is not afraid to use the subtleties of cut, drape, and tailoring to flatter, enhance, exaggerate or conceal the attributes of the wearer.
—M

American women are so proud to have gained a measure of power that they appear rough and tough. In France, this goes down badly. In the United States women took their business style from men. We did, too, a few years ago. But we understood this wasn't very feminine and did nothing for us. So now we've turned to a softer look, playing up the contrasts with men.
—Clementine Gustin, quote in *The World*

The French are often too
self-indulgent. They feel it
is so important to express
their 'personality' through
their clothes, to read people by what they wear.
— Men's Fashions of the
Times

in Paris and most major cities carry the latest immediately; there is no "trickle" effect, as in America. As soon as it's "in," it's worn by everyone—adapted, of course, to the basic style. The French don't have to wait for newspaper and magazine articles and pictures to become instantly chic. But that doesn't mean that they discard clothes. They are impresarios of adaptation. If the trend indicates change from long, tube skirts to short ones, the Frenchwoman will immediately alter hers. If acid green is "the" color, they will find a way to use it with their current wardrobe—a touch here, a touch there, and they are *au courant*.

Martine Bercu observes that American women, regardless of profession or position, tend to look similar. But in Paris, three women from the same profession will look quite distinct. It's not only a matter of looking the part, looking like they spend money on clothes, but also the flair with which they put things together.

American women, for example, wear "outfits"—matching shoes, bag, suit, and blouse. In France, the Frenchwoman takes pride in being eclectic, taking a little of this, and a little of that, to make a wonderful look. Martine calls it creative "anarchy," rather than a system of putting clothes together.

Both Italian and French women instinctively have the right touch. Numerous accessories can be spread out before them, and it's amazing the knack they possess for pulling together seemingly uncommon combinations. And they don't wear suits, per se—at least not in the American sense. They have an unerring sense of style that looks, to the casual observer, unstructured and yet appears to be very put together. (It should be noted here that French women, young and old alike, have developed a look which varies little from year to year and season to season. Whether she's preppie, classic, trendy, feminine, aristocratic, she chooses additions to her wardrobe to enhance her style and makes purchases always with that innate style in mind. She doesn't become a completely different woman with each change of wardrobe.)

While clothing is a more accurate indicator of status, investment is dictated more by income level. (There's definitely a greater disparity between the spending habits of the rich and the not-so-rich in Europe). It's a fact, however, that American women spend three times as much money on clothes than their European counterparts who prefer to buy *fewer* pieces and keep them longer.

In fact, clothes define position—the more money you make the more you are expected to spend on clothes. In France and Italy, if you make $20,000, your clothes indicate that; if you earn $70,000, your clothes reflect that, too. In America, it is sometimes difficult to tell who's who by the clothes one wears. This may be due, in part, to our flexible status system. Americans often identify socioeconomic level and status by clothes, houses, and cars.

Culture plays a significant role in determining the distinctiveness of the dress codes—from country to country and from business to business. Despite these differences, which are also hallmarks of a particular country, people who work internationally often assemble accessories and accent pieces from a mixture of many countries. All of us can adapt our look so that we blend in, whether we're in The City, the halls of Versailles, at the Hague, at La Scala. Our European friends have suggested ways that one can become an internationalist—unlike JR and Bobby Ewing who, in Russia, conducted business in their cowboy boots and Stetsons.

There are some things that work and will go a long way toward internationalizing your dress, toward making your European colleagues feel comfortable, toward preventing your clothes from getting in the way of doing business.

What works

For Men:
Narrow, cuffless trousers

Expensive ties

Lively socks

Tasseled loafers

Navy blue blazers for week-end attire

More formal dressing in Argentina

A dark suit for evening

Gold unostentatious watches

For Women:
Well-designed "significant" jewelry

A simple gold watch

Unusual combinations of pattern and color

Dressy and casual components

A black Italian shoulder bag large enough to hold files (instead of a brief-case)

Scarves to soften suits

Softly styled suits

Separates and accessories

Longer hair

For Both:
Good leather shoes, well kept

A mixture of Euro- and American designs

What doesn't work

For Men:
Brown shoes in London

Ties with bold regimental stripes on the Continent

For Women:
Very long, polished nails

Heavy makeup for day

Overly matched clothes

Overly styled hair

Light bottoms and dark tops

For Both:
Inexpensive shoes

Uncared-for shoes

International Savvy*

Do

- When conducting business, wear business clothes, even in hot weather.

- Keep jewelry at a minimum.

- Use a fountain pen.

- Do introduce people as follows:

  —learn to pronounce the names of the people you'll be introducing.

  —get titles right.

  —use an honorific when addressing a business associate; (first names are not used.)

  —say the name of the most important person first.

  —look at each person as you say his or her name.

- Shake hands on both arrival and departure.

- Shake hands with everyone in the group, starting with the oldest person or one of senior rank.

- European women shake hands with both men and women.

  —if you're a man, let a European woman extend her hand first.

- In China, the pumping hand is a sign of pleasure in the meeting.

- In Japan, an informal 15-degree bow, hands-at-the-side, followed by a hand shake.

- Discuss your personal or family life only if asked. Be discreet.

- Lower your voice.

- Listen quietly. . . and a lot.

- Nod discreetly to make a point.

- In waving goodbye, use only your fingers, not your whole arm.

- Wait until you are offered food and drink.

- Know the correct placement of utensils during, and at the end of each course.

- Learn the continental method of handling knife and fork.

- When not holding utensils, empty hands should be on the table (no elbows, please!), not in your lap.

- For American women, don't open the door if there's a man present (it's viewed as macho and aggressive.)

Don't

- Write on the back of your own or a Japanese's business card.

- Invite a European to call you by your first name until you have been well acquainted.

- In Saudi Arabia or Thailand, do not shake hands with a woman (touching a woman is a sign of disrespect.)

- Ask personal questions (they're considered too rude and too personal).

- In Moslem countries, do not ask a man about his wife.

- Use expansive gestures. (They're acceptable only in Mediterranean countries, e.g. southern Italy and Greece.)

- Use the "OK sign" to signify agreement (it's considered obscene in Brazil and a vulgar sexual invitation in Greece, Ghana, and Turkey. In France and Belgium, it means "zero" or "worthless".)

- Lead your guest (instead of following) through doors and halls.

* Adapted from "International Savvy" by Dorothea Johnson, who wrote the "International Protocol" column for the Washington World Trade Centers "Washington Trade Report".

7

Stripping Away the Superfluous

Do you shop at the last minute for that special event?

Are you an impulse buyer?

Do you wander aimlessly around a department store?

Do you face your closet every morning with dread?

Do you often complain that you have nothing to wear, even when you face a closet full of clothes?

Do you have mistakes in your closet?

Do you have clothes in your closet that you haven't worn in six months? in a year? in over two years?

When push comes to shove, do you always select the same suit? the same shirts? the same ties?

If you answered "yes" to any of the above questions, you are ready to read this chapter and to do something about the "monster in your closet." What do I mean by the "monster in your closet"? Well, if you're like many of us, you have a closet full of clothes; and you probably wear less than 1/3 of them. When you have that big meeting, when you're meeting a new associate, or when you go on an important interview, you probably choose the same special outfit.

It's the outfit you know works for you. It makes you feel confident, at your best, and gets you through almost any occasion. Maybe it's the dark navy pinstriped suit, the navy silk tie, and the white broadcloth shirt. Or maybe it's that semi-fitted black wool crepe suit with the shell pink silk blouse. Whatever yours looks like, you love it, and it has never failed you.

Style: At work it means knowing how to stand out without looking out of step.
— Self

But what about all the other clothes in your closet? There's that brown plaid suit you bought two years ago on impulse because you thought you needed a change. And that two-piece red and black dress that looked so good on the rack and was priced just right. And that marvelous fuchsia silk that looked so smart on the salesperson. What about those shirts that just don't look crisp enough, or those man-tailored blouses that make you look masculine?

In most cases, the clothes we're talking about may be perfectly good, but for one reason or another, they simply don't fit the life you live now, the person you are now, the job you have now. You've changed; they haven't. Clothes, like lives, styles, and jobs, have a season, and then, at some point, should be changed and updated.

This is especially the case if you believe that clothes send specific messages, especially so, if you realize that clothes can work for you, can do the "talking" for you, can get you into the places you want to go, and *can influence the deals you're trying to make.*

In my experience at FYI Wardrobing Service, I have worked with more men and women who had incredible wardrobes. No matter how much they spent or how much time they devoted to shopping for clothes, they still overbought and were faced with the same dilemma each morning of "what shall I wear today?"

Before I can help you put together a wardrobe that will work (no matter which category you work in and what your lifestyle), you must do something important so that you can easily assemble your daily dress, your travel wardrobe, and dress for special events. You've probably guessed what it is already. *You have to clean your closet.* That's right. You have to do the job most of us put off from year to year until we've accumulated so many items our closets and drawers are bulging at the seams.

Why start with the closet? You know the old saying—"If you don't know where you're going, any road will get you there." This also holds true for building a wardrobe; you have to begin with a plan, a plan that will provide the roadmap to spending your clothing budget wisely whether it's $100 or $1,000. To do that, you must know what you have that works and what can be the foundation for an exceptionally functional, exciting, and appropriate wardrobe.

Every morning at 7 A.M., the following exchange takes place in Brooklyn: "I have nothing to wear," she says. "You have a closetful of nothing to wear," he says. Then he marches over to his closet, flings open the door, and cries, "Now, *this* is the closet of someone with nothing to wear."
— *New York*

Closet Cleaning

So, start immediately in your closet. Most of us dread this task because our closets contain our past lives (many of us have in the back of our closet some Pakistani shirts, madras jackets, plastic clothes, 3-D glasses). Our closets also contain our wishes and fantasies—the clothes we've saved until we lose that extra ten or twenty pounds, or cocktail and party clothes that we've hardly used, but will, we fervently believe.

You'll discover much about yourself by going through your closet. You may find that you have invested heavily in fantasy more than reality—especially in the days before you hit the magic 3-0. You'll also discover that one of the major problems we have all faced most of our lives is that we have shopped without a plan. Yet, we wouldn't dream of shopping for a car or a major appliance without consulting the latest *Consumer's Digest*. But we don't often apply the same discipline to shopping for our wardrobes.

How do you get through this closet cleaning? It's easy. You're going to go through that closet and handle every single item in it. You will decide what to keep and to give away by answering two simple questions:

- Do I like it?
- Does it still perform well for me?

You're going to create three piles. The first is for the clothes that work, that fit into the way you live and work now; the second is for clothes that almost work; and the third is for those clothes that are totally wrong.

You're going to have to be pretty ruthless about this sorting process. This is serious business, and you're going to have to commit to doing what's necessary to put together an effective wardrobe. I realize it's going to be hard for some of you to consign your all-time favorites to the "give away" pile. But look on the bright side—all those "give aways" can be tax deductions, if you donate them to Goodwill or your favorite next-to-new shop or in the case of seasonless designer clothes, to a costume museum such as the Metropolitan Museum of Art's Costume Wing, the University of Minnesota's Goldstein Gallery, the Brooklyn Museum, and other outstanding costume repositories and museums.

Dressing badly indicates a certain contempt for other people, which will be forgiven only if you are very rich or very talented or simply have no social, financial, or business ambitions.
—Michael Korda, quoted in *Playboy*

Before you tackle your closet, make sure you give yourself plenty of time. Don't start the process if you are not able to complete it in one session. Choose a day, a morning, an afternoon, or an evening when you know you won't be disturbed, when you know you won't be distracted.

Before you actually get into the closet, let's discuss in some detail what "ones", "twos", and "threes" look like.

The "Ones"

Clothes in the "ones," are clothes that are always on target. These are clothes that you gravitate to for important events, and more often than not, successful events. You never feel over- or under-dressed. Often, it may even be, in your mind's eye, your "lucky" suit or dress. "Ones" are the clothes that make you look and feel successful and confident. Most of the clothes in this group transcend seasons and fashion; they are the timeless, quality garments that make up the foundation of a good business wardrobe.

The "Twos"

The "twos" are "almost" clothes. They fall short of the mark for a variety of reasons. Maybe they're almost right, but the color isn't quite right for you; or the fabric itches; or the style is wonderful, but it's not you. The "twos" also include clothes we seldom wear, and when we do, we invariably meet someone we didn't expect to. You know the feeling: you're attending an important meeting, and you don't feel quite put together; or you're out to lunch and you run into someone important you haven't seen in a while, and your immediate thought is "Why didn't I wear my dark blue suit, my favorite shirt?" Whenever you've felt you looked less than your best, you were probably wearing a "two."

So, you ask, what's the big difference between "ones" and "twos"? Probably the best way to explain is to imagine meeting a very important client, or being called to a top-level meeting, or encountering someone special unexpectedly. If you've got a "one" on, you instantly have a feeling of well being, of having a successful meeting. If it's a "two," you'll know exactly what you should have worn, and you'll even find yourself retreating from front and center because you know you're not at your best.

Do you remember how you felt the last time you wore a "two" and saw a familiar and important associate? You hid behind the cereal rack in the supermarket or behind the plumbing supplies in the hardware store. Any maneuver to avoid meeting that person while looking like "this"!

The "Threes"

Out and out mistakes are "threes"—clothes that don't work at all. They don't for a variety of reasons; they're dated, the fabric doesn't wear well. For most of us, the "threes" are the clothes we bought on impulse because we felt we had to buy "something," or because it was a bargain too good to pass up, or because we were depressed or, conversely, elated. The "threes" are also the result of distaste for shopping. Because we hate to do it, we get it done as quickly as possible, without much thought. Often, the "threes" haven't seen the light of day for months, even years—yet they take up space in our closets.

Nostalgia Clothes

A fourth category I label "nostalgia" clothes. These clothes that evoke special memories, and for that reason, we can't bear to part with them. If you have some apparel or accessories like that, get them out of your closet and into a storage trunk. The kids will love them years from now—and so will you! Now that you have a clear understanding of what constitutes a "one," a "two," or a "three," you're ready to begin.

Closet Cleaning Made Simple

You're going to make three separate piles: Put the "ones" and "twos" on the bed or large table, the "threes" on the floor. Go ahead; you've got to begin somewhere. Take each item out of the closet. Carefully examine it. Decide whether you like it, and then put it to the final test by asking yourself does it work well for me? Now assign it to one of the three piles. Once you have examined each piece and

Put clothes into piles: 1s, 2s, and 3s.

put it in the appropriate pile, then, look at those piles. Really look! You'll have some remarkable insights.

First, you'll probably recognize why you had a closet full of clothes and still felt you had nothing to wear. When they are all piled together, you'll see that the "ones" have a certain level of quality, design, and color that is far superior to the "twos." Then, you'll notice how much you've changed, because your "twos" and "threes" no longer reflect your values, your emotions, the life you live now. You'll see choices of color, pattern, and shape you liked when you were first married, or when you moved from a Northern state to a Southern climate. You'll see your past reflected there. Along with your clothes, you have grown and changed. You'll be dismayed to find that a good percentage of the "twos" and "threes" are almost like new, but don't work well for you now. Simply summed up, you've changed; your clothes haven't!

Double check each pile. Go through each pile again, double-checking your first evaluation so you're positive you've made the right move. At this stage, you'll probably find that you move some more "ones" into the "twos" pile. This second pass is also a good time to check the "ones" for repair and cleaning needs. As you put each "one" back into the closet, check the appropriate category in the inventory at the end of this chapter. Make sure you leave nothing out because this inventory will become the basis for new purchases and the wardrobing principles we'll be outlining in the next chapter.

Most of us like to think of ourselves as pretty savvy. We know good investments when we see them—the common stock that's on its way up, the small enterprise that's headed for big things, the automobile that's worth its price, the house that will appreciate with time. But nowhere do we seem to be less savvy than in the investment we make in clothes.

And there are several reasons for this. One major reason is that most of us increasingly lack time to shop and time to study fashion. Another reason is that stores are bigger and more complicated to shop. Often, departments are moved overnight; what you saw yesterday is gone today. Some people even lose their bearings in some large stores!

At the same time that stores are becoming more complicated and less user friendly, fashion itself is moving fast, changing in mood and shape, crossing international boundaries, and mixing in a most sophisticated way. All of this is going on when your time is more limited, more precious.

Just look at the piles of "twos" and "threes." Add up the cost of them. If you were to calculate their current worth, you'd be surprised to find out just how much you invested in clothes that simply don't give you value for your money because they don't work for you as they should. Even the most practical people will find that they have invested over $3,000 or more in "twos" and "threes" that they're dissatisfied with. And just as you have to sell stocks that no longer provide value, change automobiles when they become a liability, you've got to get the "twos" and "threes" out of your wardrobes.

List remaining clothes on Inventory at back of book.

Now, with the inventory at hand, take another look in your closet. Try on all the garments to determine what fits and what doesn't, and what needs to be altered, if that's an option. If you must, get rid of the "ones" that need too much alteration to make them work; it's not worth it. What remains will now form the basic wardrobe for all the future decisions you make regarding new purchases over the next few months, and even into the next few years. This objective look will tell you what is lacking in your wardrobe, what needs filling out, what needs restocking, what completely new purchases you need and what you simply "must have" to be appropriately dressed to go anywhere or meet anyone, even at the last minute.

Now, with that arduous and often painful task over (it's tough to give away an old friend!), you're ready to embark on the next phase—wardrobing to maximize the potential in your closet.

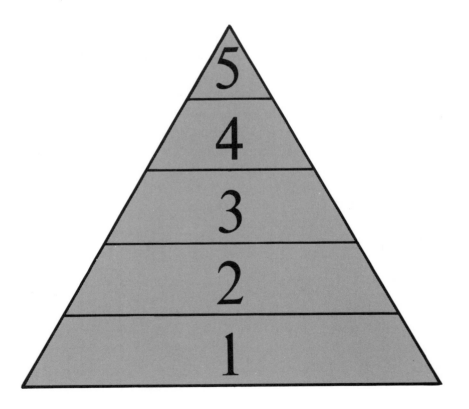

8

Pyramid Control

Just as you want your investments to do more for you, so too must your wardrobe investment pay the same dividends. You've cleaned your closet and the only items remaining are those which are appropriate for your current business and social lifestyle. They work well, look well, and fit well for the kind of job you have, the industry you're in, and the company culture that influences your choices.

We all know the price of good clothes. In recent years, the escalation is enough to stagger even the most affluent, but a good working wardrobe does not have to cost a small fortune. So whether your annual budget for clothes is $800, $1,500, or $2,500, you can go shopping and get the most for that budget.

Wardrobing by Stages

The key is planning—what I call the "Pyramid" concept. It divides wardrobing into five stages, beginning with building a workable base wardrobe (Stage One) to spending your whole budget on one or two key items (Stage Five). And Pyramiding works, whether you're in Category I, II, or III.

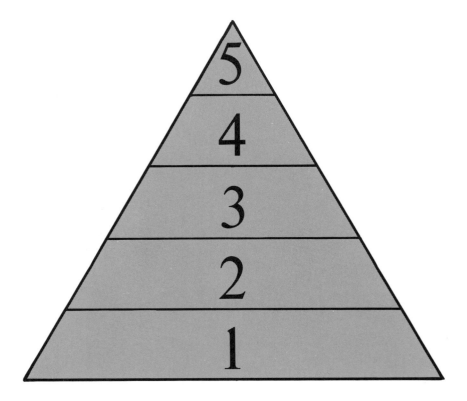

But before we talk about spending your budget at the various stages, let's take a look at what constitutes a complete wardrobe. You've discovered your favorite base colors, the styling appropriate for your Category, and have determined the life you lead (what you do, where you do it—daily, weekly, monthly, and yearly). Now let's really dig in.

In the following discussions, you'll discover that most of the clothes and accessories you wear fall into four major groupings:

Backgrounds

Simple clothes can take all-out accessorizing: The dress should be a backdrop. In some cases, a little goes a long way. —Isabel Canovas, quoted in *Vogue*

These are the clothes that serve as a backdrop for accessories and other clothing. Often, they are simple in silhouette and neutral in color. Suits, shirts, blouses, dresses, and jackets can be the background elements in your wardrobe. What you choose to wear with these pieces are the items which give your outfits distinction and reflect your personality.

Pivots

A pivot is one key item that everything revolves around, that everything goes with. It can be a jacket in a multi-color tweed, a paisley blouse, or a patterned scarf. Pivots are especially good choices in Stages One and Two because they enable you to expand a minimal wardrobe in such a way that you always look put together, always look as though you are wearing something that was designed to work together. Pivots blend with your basic pieces so that your look seems ever-changing. Pivots are items that you will wear often because they work with almost every other item in your wardrobe.

Signature pieces

Signature pieces become associated with you; they mark your personal style. Like the way you sign your name, it is uniquely yours. Signatures are so distinctive, that they make a definitive statement. It can be a piece of jewelry, a ring or watch, or cufflinks. Certain pieces which strike you become the "signature" of your style.

Signatures take your wardrobe out of the ordinary. For example, a woman might be taken with a Japanese patterned blouse — a blouse with a combination of colors and pattern so subtle it gives her an individual look every time she wears it. This blouse, like all signatures, is distinctive; it's a personalized imprint of your style which appears throughout your wardrobe. You can put it inside your basic suit, and it becomes a striking accessory. You can wear it open with a camisole and short skirt for a cocktail event. You can wear it with a pair of slacks, and you have a totally different look. All the other pieces are background, and they determine what you're doing when you team them with your signature piece.

A signature grows out of what comes naturally — your style and personality. You may consciously choose a signature, but unless it's an extension of the real you, it will look like a costume.
— Glamour

Accents

Accents are the little details — scarves, jewelry, belts — that give a finished look to whatever you're wearing. They're the pieces designers use in their runway shows to make the clothes look spectacular, that make the design significant, that get buyers to take another look. These accents, or accessories, enhance very simple clothing because they create a spectacular look. They are the main threads that update your wardrobe from season to season.

Most women of the baby boom generation went from blue jeans to blue suits. They went from one uniform to another. They've spent years competing in a man's world, and now they're rediscovering their femininity. This is their first brush with dressing up.

—Laura Sinderbrand, quoted in Newsweek

9
Smart Women, Smart Choices

The Evolution of Women's Dress

When I moved from the world of art and design into the world of business, I became more and more aware of what I like to call the "Invisible Woman."

There she was filling her role as an ornament or a token. And there, in her working background, very identifiable, were men. Powerful men. Despite the fact that there were over 57% women in the workforce, many holding key positions, why didn't we see her? Why was the balance of power in the male court? What factors contributed to keeping women in subordinate positions or somehow so vague as to seem invisible?

It was not then, and is not, today, difficult to recognize the power and authority of the male executive. Part of this awareness stems from the subconscious message his clothing sends—a message everyone understands—but women's does not.

Men's clothing signals power, position, and freedom of movement. It's functional, neat, and clearly understood. Many times it gives the wearer much more than he has on his own. Numerous signals like the tie, with its color, shape, and design, act as identifying symbol of rank. The tie, along with color of the suit (suit as opposed to sport jacket), wing-tip soft-soled shoes, cuffs-no cuffs—all denote position and job I.D.

If the suit makes the man, so it must be that the suit makes the woman. Or so young female executives of the seventies must have reasoned as they toiled their way toward the boardroom bound up in gray flannel skirts, oxford cloth shirts, and little bow ties. A decade later, as they began to break through the "invisible ceiling" into upper management, they cast off those "yuppie suits" in favor of more feminine attire.
— *Vogue*

Women have adopted the clothing of male colleagues in the workplace in order to appropriate its expressive qualities. They imitate in pursuit of a social object: acceptance as a competent and equal partner in the world of work. Imitation is devoted to acquiring the symbolic complements in which competence and equality are expressed. Imitation then is not the simple pursuit of prestige, not the work of some generalized force; it is a culturally purposeful activity motivated by an appreciation of the symbolic liabilities of one style of dress, and the symbolic advantages implied in another.
— *The Psychology of Fashion*

Women's clothing did none of that. It was soft, flowered, cute or sexy, or very kid-casual. Typical women's symbols—high heels, slim-fitting skirts, short skirts, fragile fabrics, and soft light colors—inhibit movement, express a certain fragility, and a hands-off attitude. Beautiful, but restrictive. These symbols didn't imply *action*. Recognizing the need for "power" symbols, women began to adapt and appropriate male symbols. Enter the pinstriped man-tailored suit, the shirt, and the floppy bow tie. (A great deal of this adaptation was on a subconscious level, but it happened *en masse*.)

It was this language of a business which got her in, much as dressing like a tomboy got girls into the boy's club. (I always thought the tomboy was smart. I was one and I loved it, not realizing my "link" was jeans and dad's shirt. But what I loved about the dress was not being "like a boy,"—because naturally I wasn't—but being an insider, a member of this exciting, "secret" male society. Most of all I loved the freedom of their dress. I could move, stretch, sit anywhere and anyway I wanted. And when I played baseball, I looked even better dirty.)

Because of all that, "business dress" took women out of the sidelines (just as it does the tomboy), and put her right into the middle of it all.

Why, when our dress changed, could we suddenly look like we could do a man's as well as a woman's job? It was the freedom-of-movement implication, but it was also a borrowed set of symbols which were, and continue to be, boring and lacking in individuality because women aren't men and don't want to be! They wanted what the clothing denoted—freedom, responsibility, position identification, power—an appearance of competency.

During that period, I once made a comment about women being motivated differently because they were different. A vice president in that meeting said, vis-a-vis equality, "We could get sued for saying that." And that was part of the struggle in business and within women. Somehow equal meant "we are the same." Today, different is not seen as more than or less than.

Much of that earlier thinking can possibly be attributed to how little many organizations valued women's behavior, thinking processes, and business methods. We began adapting (like immigrants surviving in a hostile land) the version of the male uniform.

Over the last few years, we have further adapted it, and now, more effectively than ever, we are learning to blend it with decidedly female symbols.

Business now has a new respect for women's intuition, sensitivity, concern for morale, and subtle perceptions. Her way of thinking, of making connections, are the very traits that have come to be valued, maybe because it was time, or more likely, because of the influence of so many women in all fields of business.

What was for a period exciting and strong—the man-tailored suit, shirt and bow-tie—is now regarded passé in some industries and professions. The suit remains (and thank goodness it does, because it is the garment of position and strength), but it's being softened by a simply designed or elegant blouse in subtle or vibrant color, by interesting scarves, and pins.

The business dress, too, has made a successful entree into the work world. It's a woman's business symbol and a welcome change from the suit. But it has an identity that connotes business and is a successful *counterpart* of the suit. It is often a well-designed piece that lends itself to a multitude of accessory options. Women finally have a wide variety of choices that work well because they have worked through specific adaptations of the significant male business symbols and they have established their presence visibly as counterparts as well as equals with their own female position symbols.

In other words, women became VISIBLE.

The Compleat Business Wardrobe

Many of you probably have the base components described below in your newly cleaned closet. Let's see how the "ones" you chose fit into the base needed to take you from a formal business meeting to a weekend at your boss's house in the Hamptons to a two-week business trip at home or abroad.

Suits and Jackets

The cornerstone of a functional business wardrobe is a suit plus an extra jacket. Whether you work in a Category I, II, or III organization, you should have, at Stage One, one suit and one extra jacket. This suit can be in any variety of styles—from the lapeled jacket

For the modern, intelligent working woman, dressing for success means choosing clothes that suit her environment and express her personal style, mixing costly and inexpensive pieces, old and new elements, to create a look that reflects her taste and attitude. We've always found there are no rules. As women become more confident about their abilities, they wear what they want to wear.
—Patricia Matson, quoted in *Elle*

(either notched- or shawl-collared) to a V-necked tailored or box jacket, to a cardigan with soft shoulders. This suit is beautifully tailored with clean, simple lines. It can be made up in a gabardine or wool crepe, and preferably in a neutral color. Neutrals that work best for this background suit are black, navy, taupe, gray, pewter, or camel. These are colors that interchange easily, or can be separated and work with the other items to give you the variety of outfits needed in Stage One. If you're in a relaxed Category II or Category III organization, you can probably choose your favorite, non-traditional color for this background suit. Non-traditional colors include mauve, bronze, and loden green.

Because a suit is the basis for all the choices you make in your wardrobe and because it will be with you a long time, you need to choose one that really looks well on you and one that fits into the culture of your organization.

If you're in a Category I company, this base suit should be more structured and more traditional. If you're in a Category II company where there's a little more room for personal expression, you can choose suits with more relaxed lines, more exaggerated detail. A Chanel or softly styled cardigan suit might be a good choice here. These styles can also be chosen for later stages in a Category I environment. A good Category III suit might be more unstructured, less classic in design.

The second item in your base wardrobe is an extra jacket. This could be a traditional jacket or sweater jacket that coordinates with your base suit. Good choices for this item are a shaped jacket which is loosely styled or subtly patterned or a handsome cardigan jacket. If you choose the cardigan jacket, it can either be the long variety or the newer, cropped cardigan. For a dressier look you might select a sweater jacket in a luxurious knit. One choice is a long sleeved, hip length, collarless knit in a striking, multi-colored pattern that picks up all the colors in your wardrobe. Another possibility is a patterned weave in mohair. Any of these jackets can be combined and coordinated with the skirts described below.

(Specific suit styles and shapes for each Category are outlined at the end of this Chapter.)

Skirts

To add versatility and flexibility, you need three skirts:
- one short black skirt that will work with either the suit jacket or the extra jacket.
- one long, pleated skirt for a more upscale, dressy look.
- a paisley gathered (dirndl) skirt.

When you're selecting these skirts, look for colors that work with the base suit and jacket. For example, if your base suit is black and your extra jacket a jewel-toned purple in a single-breasted jacket, you might want to select a short, black gabardine skirt, a long, pleated black skirt in a wool blend, and a charcoal gray/cream paisley dirndl skirt. I stress again that it's important to choose skirts of the best quality, as well as in colors that complement and coordinate with your base pieces. Your selection should always be made with an eye to how it extends the wearability of the pieces you already own. Your goal is to have them tastefully coordinate so that they take you to work, to an after-hours business function, or even to a cocktail party.

Blouses

Blouses give your suits, jackets, and skirts a finished look. If you select them with handsome detailing, they can make even the fewest of base pieces look new and fresh. Sometimes blouses can be the items that set your wardrobe apart—that take the humdrum out of even the most conservative business looks.

To achieve that special look, that individuality, you should have a minimum of eight blouses or blouse substitutes. Because your blouse is a key element in extending your wardrobe, always ask yourself before making a purchase: How will this particular blouse work with what I already have? You will find that some blouse choices will be background; others will be signatures.

What kinds of blouses help create this versatility? For starters, you'll need one dressy blouse in a satin, a silk-on-silk, or a silk in white or off-white, the latter in shades of ivory, champagne, oyster, or cream (white, or off-white, helps to pull outfits together and goes with just about anything you wear).

A good choice might be white satin with a softly rounded neckline, beautiful sleeves, and a softly gathered bodice. It can be worn

The collective vision of the successful executive woman once was having it all—a sexy superwoman in a mink coat and sunglasses with a baby cradled in one arm and a crocodile briefcase on her lap, talking on a car phone in her limousine. That image of the businesswoman as invincible Uber-dame has had it.

Gone, too, is the aura of unimpeachable assertiveness that once surrounded her spiritual ancestor, the power-suited clone who cloaked her femininity in mannish tailoring and a little bow tie, unshakably convinced that getting ahead in business meant imitating her male boss detail for detail.
—*Elle*

with either of the solid skirts for dressy occasions, such as an after-hours meeting, or dinner party, or a fashionable luncheon. For an equally dressy look, but one with a bit more distinction, you might select a long-sleeve, silk-on-silk blouse with a standup or Mandarin collar, geometric breast pockets set off with brass buttons. Add gold chains à la Chanel, and voilà, you have a Euro-blouse. This will go to dinner anywhere in the world.

The second blouse should be what I call a "mid-level" blouse. It has either a jewel neckline or convertible collar which can be worn up or down, open or closed and serves as background for accessories. This blouse does not call attention to itself, but turns your basic suit into an ensemble. A shell with cap sleeves in a neutral would also fit this mid-level category.

Next, you'll want to have a lapeled casual shirt. This can be a solid or stripe in a non-shiny fabric that can be worn with skirts alone, can fit under the suit, or, for a more casual look, can be worn open at the neck with slacks. These three blouses will serve you for business, casual, and dress events.

Your next choice should be a handsome linen camp shirt. Again, the idea here is to choose one which can be worn with any of the items so that when you change your blouse, you change your look.

Sweaters add another dimension to one's wardrobe. For that reason, I suggest you add three. The first should be a sweater blouse—a refined, finished sweater with either a jewel neckline or a turtle-neck. This could be a signature piece—a piece that can be worn with your suit for business or paired with one of your skirts to take you comfortably to a cocktail party. This particular sweater might be a designer number edged in black with a special bow trim. Team it with a little black knit skirt, and you have just added a knit dress to your wardrobe.

Next, you'll want to include a tunic sweater, perhaps in a jewel color. It will go with all of the skirts, either belted or unbelted. You'll also want to include a casual oversized "fun" sweater in textured yarns and playful color combinations to wear with slacks. This sweater works great for company picnics, barbecues, or casual at-home get-togethers (if you work for a company where Fridays are less formal than the other days of the week, this sweater might be a perfect solution).

And last but not least is a camisole. It can worn with a variety of skirt and jacket or skirt and sweater combinations for the cocktail circuit. This is an especially good purchase if you attend numerous fairly dressy functions after work and don't have time to go home to change. Simply wear the camisole under your blouse during the day, remove the blouse, change your jewelry, and depending on the dressiness of the occasion, wear, or leave off, the jacket, and you're ready for cocktails.

Dresses

Because the acceptance of women in the executive ranks of almost every business is more universal today, it is no longer necessary that women mirror their male counterparts by wearing the uniform suit. And because so many woman have entered the workforce in recent years, they have progressed a long way in softening cliché dress attitudes. Two things have resulted. A woman's dress is differentiated from a man's, and symbols that are expressly feminine and female have been developing. The dress is the primary example; jewelry and bags another.

In recent years, the market has understood this feminization and has begun to include good-looking, well-designed dresses for the business woman. Dresses, like suits, can define your look without diminishing your perceived level or position. How many dresses form the working woman's wardrobe options? Seven.

A business dress, often a coat dress in gabardine, is a good first choice. Here again, the look should be classic, the cut impeccable, and the color neutral. This dress can be worn on its own or paired with jackets and/or blouses to effectively change a look. If, for instance, you've built your base wardrobe around black, then a camel, taupe, or khaki coat dress can work well under your black jacket. And if it is loosely fitted, it can be worn as a "duster" over skirt and blouse, as well as alone with a choice of accessories. If it's black, it goes well with a tuxedo look and easily takes you from day to evening.

Knits too, are a simple solution for day-into-evening dressing. That's why I recommend purchasing a two-piece knit, simply styled, and complementary in color to the other pieces in your wardrobe. Knits form an extremely functional part of a wardrobe and can give you a suit look. Designer Mary Jane Marcasiano, in an article in

Black is like no other color. It is at once sexy and refined, romantic and cool. To American women, black is the ticket to sophistication. . . . Black carries with it a long, rich history. It has been worn by religious orders since ancient times. It was the color for mourning as early as the 14th century. And in literature and the arts, black has always been a powerful symbol.

Consider, for instance, the great portraits by such artists as Rubens and Valazquez, Manet and Sargent. The two that always stick in my mind are Manet's painting of Berthe Morisot and Sargent's "Madame X." How hauntingly beautiful these women looked in black.

As for novels, would Vronsky have fallen in love with Anna Karenina at that fateful ball? . . . It was her low-cut black velvet gown that made all the difference. And let us not forget Scarlett O'Hara. After the death of poor Charles Hamilton, her first husband, convention dictated

Vogue, says of knits, "They're so incredible to wear and easy to travel in. . . . They feel good, look good, and go from day to dinner."

Today, there's a wide range to choose from; you can select from such haute couture European designers as Yves St. Laurent and Missoni to bridge American designers Adrienne Vittadini, Linda Allard for Ellen Tracy, and Joan Vass. For daytime dressing, you can anchor your two-piece knit with a leather belt and understated accessories. For evening, you can replace the leather belt with a matching cummerbund and crystal jewelry, and you're ready for a party.

Along with the two-piece knit, you'll want a two-piece silk, a silk blend, or a challis in a foulard or a small geometric print, a stripe, a small all-over polka dot, or pin dot. This dress provides the same kind of versatility as the knit two-piecer. The top can go under your basic suit, or it can be coordinated with your extra jacket. Now, you have effectively created at least three new looks.

When choosing either of these two-piece dresses, it's important that they blend in pattern, color, and shape with what's already in your wardrobe. The two-piece concept extends that basic suit and jacket you've started out with and maximizes the versatility and coordination of your wardrobe. If you're attending a formal business meeting, you can pair the silk two-piecer with the jacket and add key accessories. Then, if you have a fashionable dinner or after-hours business event on the same day, you can remove the jacket, put on evening jewelry, and be ready to go.

It's also a good idea to have a Day/Evening dress in your wardrobe. This is the dress that looks just as right in the office with a jacket, understated jewelry, or scarf as it does with a string of pearls at a business event sans jacket. The most practical choice in this category is a simply-cut, classic, black dress. No matter where you are or who you're seeing, you cannot go wrong with black. You can take it almost anywhere in the world with a passel of accessories. Yes, the "little black dress" will always be a key piece in the wardrobe. So remember, when you're just starting out, this dress is *de rigueur* until you can afford to spend your clothing budget on more lavishly designed evening dresses.

Next, you'll want to include a real dinner dress. The design should be understated and simple, so you won't grow weary of wearing it over and over again. You might choose a dress in a simple crepe or georgette, with a jewel neckline and long set-in sleeves. A good example is a dress that has gentle pin-tucking starting just under the bosom and running to the hip line. What decides the "level" of dress is the jewelry. I suggest dramatic dull-surfaced, colored, plastic shapes for a small dinner party. For a dressier look, wear gold and/or pearls. And for a really major event, opt for crystal or diamonds. Because the line and design of your dress is so simple, it can take you to any city, here or abroad.

Then, for those really important and/or gala events, you'll want to have a cocktail dress and a celebration dress. For the cocktail dress, your first purchase can be striking, in either a low cut or strapless design. The best colors are champagne and pewter to fuchsia and emerald because they complement many types of accessories. A cocktail dress might be a signature piece.

Lastly, you'll want to include a "celebration" or special event dress. This one-of-a-kind might be in a striking color in chiffon or glitter and in a draped, or simple flowing fabric. This dress will become a signature piece.

Outerwear

In a really good working wardrobe, I suggest three coats:
- an all-weather coat
- a dress coat
- a trans-seasonal coat in gabardine

Because coats represent a sizable investment, it's important to buy high quality, classic shapes in colors which are basic or neutral. The most classic styles are wrap coats and single- or double-breasted Chesterfields (without the velvet collar) or the newer Caulfield coat. Avoid fads or current fashion statements for your first purchase.

Be aware that your coat must accommodate a suit under it; if it's too fitted, its use will be marginal. In addition to fit, check to see that full-length coats are long enough to cover all your suits and dresses. It's better to have a longer length, no matter what the skirt length.

Who Gets the Best Table?

However svelte and understated, women in pants don't command prominent tables at restaurants with corporate clientele, agreed two-thirds of upscale restauranteurs . . . polled from LA, DC, Philly, and New Orleans.

The business lunch is cause for conservative think, confirms Paul Kovi, co-owner of The Four Seasons in New York. It's a planned directed moment to get something across. . . .
—*Working Woman*

Casualwear

You do more than go to work daily, and your wardrobe should reflect the amount of time you spend in casual activities. Generally, casualwear should be chosen in two categories: dressy and rough. If you're just starting out, you'll need two pairs of slacks and one skirt. These will take you shopping on Saturday morning, to a barbecue Saturday afternoon, or to an informal dinner party. Select colors that will coordinate with the other pieces in your wardrobe. The best fabric choices are gabardine, wool crepe, or flannel.

In either category—dressy or rough—you can really splurge on color, pattern, and shape. If you want to dress down the slacks, choose shirts with patch pockets and soft shapes, in cottons and rayons.

Accents: Accessories

Accessories—belts, jewelry, scarves, bags, and shoes—define your style. They pull ensembles together and coordinate separates, and can give a lift to an otherwise limited wardrobe, especially when you have to wear the same items over and over again. Accessories raise the whole level of your wardrobe—from ordinary to extraordinary. For example, if you choose an expensive silk Yves St. Laurent shawl, you've suddenly upgraded even the most basic of suits or dresses. If you include "wearable art" in your jewelry collection, you inevitably create a look that is individual and distinctive. And remember that accessories, whenever possible, should be the best that you can afford—whether you're buying them at Stage One or Five.

Jewelry

What works best? *Real* jewelry. And you can, over the years, develop a good collection. Your first pieces should be simple designs in all gold or silver, or both. Shape is important so that you can combine pieces to complement each other. You want the mix to blend, just as your clothing does. When choosing costume jewelry, what would be nice to include are "wearable art" designs. Other wise choices in the costume jewelry category are bold or unexpected metals, unusual shapes, and interesting colors. It is important, however, to concentrate your initial investment in gold or silver.

Whose Speech Holds Your Attention? Better red, they said: Suits and dresses in dramatic colors rivet audience interest, agree four out of seven directors of prominent speakers' bureaus. A rich nourishing "feeling" color gives the audience a place to rest their eyes, confirms Kate Rand, *Working Woman's* editor-at-large, and a veteran speech giver. Color power counts.
— *Working Woman*

Accessories have a longer life span than clothing. If you succeed in matching things that are not supposed to match, then it's much more exciting.
— Paloma Picasso, quoted in *Vogue*

Some pieces you'll want to acquire as base pieces include the best quality watch, preferably in gold, in a clean, simple shape. You'll also probably want a bracelet, one that conforms to your arm. Be sure, however, that it doesn't jangle—you don't want to attract attention. As to ring choices, it's a good idea to limit one per hand. Your ring can be an heirloom of stones, but never should it be an overwhelming cocktail ring.

Earrings can be classic or creatively novel (but not bizarre) to take you from day to evening in Stage One. Earrings that dangle are best left for after-hours or in Category III businesses. Collars of gold or silver are good choices, as are chains. Heirloom or antique-looking pins work well in most businesses. At this writing, hand-made wearable art created with wit and humor is an excellent accent.

A couple of well-chosen accessories can do a lot to update your wardrobe. A shawl-sized scarf is as stylish as can be, and is often as warm as a coat. A Chanel-belt may seem expensive, but it could change the look of everything you own . . . True, this casual chic tends not to be cheap, but it adds a new layer to fashion that is eminently wearable.
—*Fashions of the Times*

Shoes

Your feet are your foundation, so it's a good idea to invest in good quality leather shoes. How your feet feel affects your well-being throughout the day. If your shoes are uncomfortable, you will be uncomfortable; you may, therefore, find yourself feeling out of sorts and possibly cancelling afternoon meetings. Shoes must be well made and must fit well.

In selecting shoes, it's a good idea to evaluate the level of movement in your daily life to determine heel height. If you do a lot of walking, you might want to choose lower heels; if you spend most of your time in your office at a desk, then you might choose a higher heel.

Classic accessories never go out of style and never look out of place—they set the standards by which others are judged.
—*Mirabella*

Simple and neutral, classically styled leather shoes are a good investment. And regardless of your level of movement, three pairs of shoes are essential in your wardrobe:
- one pair of 2 to 2-1/2 inch pumps in a color which works with your primary pieces
- one pair of dress flats
- one pair of evening shoes (sandals, sling backs, or a closed toe silk or peau de soie pump)

Scarves

Designers put a surprising amount of design creativity into scarves or shawls. Pattern and color are carefully thought out in this small, but highly important accessory. Scarves are accent pieces which pull a wardrobe together. They can "control" colors which, when worn together, might otherwise look odd until the scarf is added. Then, everything melds beautifully. Scarves can change your look from day to evening, from very business-like to dressy to casual.

They come in a variety of shapes and sizes: rectangles, diagonals, squares and oblongs. Oblongs are perhaps the most versatile. These can be worn around your neck tied as a bow, tucked into the collar ascot-style, or worn around your waist. The choice of fabric in a scarf and how you wear it determines your level of dressing.

For low-key day looks, I like foulard woolens or cotton challis scarves worn with sweaters or under jackets. For a slightly dressier look, I like silk scarves in subtle paisleys. And for a really dressy look, I suggest brilliant, multi-colored silk scarves to complement and set off an evening ensemble.

Shawls

Shawls not only add drama and color to a wardrobe, they also add warmth. In various weights and fabrics, they're wonderful choices. As with scarves, the way you wear them determines your level of dressing. In a Category I environment, you can wear your shawl tucked into the neckline of your coat. In Categories II and III, you might drape the shawl outside your coat. Shawls can also be worn draped over dresses and suits. In Category I, the draping is more controlled (you might even choose to anchor the shawl with a pin). In Categories II and III, it's draped over your shoulders and loosely knotted, or reversed with the point in front, the ends over the shoulder and down the back. For casualwear, shawls can be draped sarong-like and knotted around the waist, over slacks or skirts.

Belts

Belts give a finished look to your outfit. Your skirts and blouses come "together." Even a simple knit becomes distinctive—all with the addition of a carefully chosen belt. A belt can take you from day to evening, from season to season, even from trend to trend.

It's important, then, to have two or three belts in your wardrobe. The simple leather in a neutral is a necessary constant. Next, you can choose an interesting "rustic" belt, something in metal and leather, for a more casual look. For evening socializing, a fabric belt in a dull satin dressed up with a glittery buckle can take your Day/Evening dress to the opera mid-week, to a cocktail party, or to an intimate dinner party.

The illustrations on the following pages give you some examples of what is appropriate for Business Dress in Categories I, II, and III. Note the accessories and the interchangeability of the pieces.

Category I:
Business

Category II:
Business

Category III:
Business

These illustrations show the range of Casual dressing for Categories I, II, and III. Once again, notice how the look is pulled together with accessories.

Category I:
Casual

Category II:
Casual

Category III:
Casual

Evening dressing gives you a chance for more options—from the understated elegance of Category I to the creative trouser-smoking-jacket combination of Category III. Notice, too, that in each category, there is a version of the "little black dress."

Category I:
Evening

Category II:
Evening

Category III:
Evening

Now that you've had a look at the variety possible in all three Categories, let's explore Pyramid dressing stage by stage.

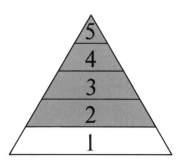

Stage One: Starting Out

Those of you just beginning your careers will probably be on a relatively limited budget. You have already eliminated the "twos" and "threes" in your closet: clothes which worked perfectly well at college but don't work in the business world, or clothes which once were appropriate for someone who worked in the home. If this is where you're starting, Stage One wardrobing is for you. Whether your annual clothing budget is $800, $1,500, or $2,500, you'll be developing a base that will give you options and flexibility. Whether you're going to a high level business event, off to the country, or on a two-week business trip, you'll have the appropriate clothes in your closet.

What do you need to start out or reenter?

- One year-round suit in gabardine or wool crepe in a solid, basic color. The lines should be classically tailored.
- Five blouses—dressy, mid-level, casual, a camisole, and a sweater blouse. The most versatile are in solid colors: off-white, pewter, bone, or soft peach. They should be simple in shape and design to work as a background for accessories.
- One casual, fun sweater in a bold pattern and wonderful texture.
- One extra jacket or sweater-jacket in a subtle pattern or texture. The jacket should be easy to wear and blend with the color tones of your basic suit.
- One extra skirt in black, either short or mid-calf.
- One pair of slacks in a solid, dark color in gabardine for year-round use. It can be worn with some of the pieces at this Stage to fill in the casualwear pieces in your wardrobe.
- One two-piece dress in a subtle patterned silk or challis, or a solid knit, in a simple silhouette with no obvious detail.
- One Day/Evening dress, possibly in black, in a knit with a soft skirt and simple neckline to serve as a background for accessories.
- Accessories to serve as accents or pivots. Choose one shawl, two scarves, two day/evening necklaces, two pairs of day/evening earrings, and two belts.

- Two pairs of shoes, one a 2" to 2 1/2" pump for day and one pair of flat shoes to wear with trousers and longer skirts.
- One day/evening coat in a dark solid, possibly a wrap.

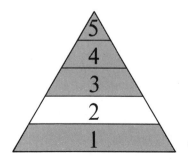

Stage Two: Adding Distinction

Once you've acquired the basics of Stage One, you're ready to spend your next budgeted allowance to add to this base. At Stage Two, your choices can become a little more distinctive. Jackets can have a more distinct pattern, shape, and color to complement your existing basics. Skirts can add a striking note and provide a welcome change to your original purchases.

The additions you'll want to purchase include:

- One additional suit, either shaped or in a patterned fabric. An excellent choice might be a multi-colored basket weave in a Chanel-style with grosgrain edging—one that goes with any color blouse.
- One patterned silk jacket which works with the base colors in your wardrobe.
- One additional skirt, perhaps a pleated wool crepe, to coordinate with the new jacket.
- Two blouses. One a signature blouse with detailed accents or a significant pattern. Here, you can add unusual colors and prints or patterns and stripes in a variety of fabrics—challis, cotton, linen, silk, and silk blends. The second blouse, in an off-white or chalk white, will freshen up the basics you purchased in Stage One. Now is the time to include more expensive blouses.
- One business dress in a gabardine or knit. The style should be subtle, yet distinctive.
- One dinner dress to take you to many functions. It should be well-designed so you never tire of it.
- Two additional casual tops, one dressy and one roughwear. If you choose sweaters, you might look for a fine knit with classic detail and a big pullover such as a Shaker or fisherman knit for those days out-of-doors.
- One roughwear pair of trousers in denim, khaki, poplin, or twill.
- One pair of leather shoes in subtle pattern or design.
- One signature accessory or, the alternative, jewelry in gold or silver.

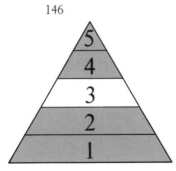

Stage Three: Panache

At this stage of wardrobing, you can finally purchase what you want. You've got the basics plus wardrobe extenders, and now you can shop with an eye to more styling and panache than to functionality. You can introduce key pieces from favorite Euro-designers (Claude Montana, Perry Ellis, Isaac Mizrahi, Romeo Gigli, Donna Karan) and accessories and blouses.

Here's what you can add to your wardrobe at this stage:

- One knock-out suit in silk in a distinctive shape and color.
- One jacket, perhaps in an intriguing pattern and elongated design. This jacket can serve as a signature jacket. It becomes associated with you and your overall style.
- One fairly expensive "background" blouse to update those you already have.
- One cocktail dress in black or solid color in a simply styled designer number.
- One sophisticated casual outfit in a distinctive color, pattern, and shape.
- One pair of evening shoes.
- Dramatic accessories: For example, signature shapes in crystal, jet, or solid gold collar necklaces, or a wide bangle bracelet, or an alligator handbag.

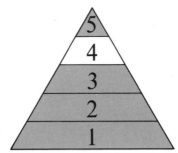

Stage Four: Self-indulgence

Now that you've progressed this far and have a wardrobe that you feel absolutely confident in because it goes anywhere, you can afford to shop for what you really want. You know the feeling—you saw that dress, that coat, that suit—and you've just got to have it! And at this stage, you really *can* have it. You have made shopping in the past an investment in the basics. Now, you can afford to take a flyer; you can splurge. And at this stage, you know what works for you and works with the wardrobe you've been accumulating.

Now, you'll be looking for replacements and for new items. Here's a list of the pieces you'll want to consider adding:

- One replacement or additional suit. This should be a good designer suit that is background in color, but very distinctive in shape.

- One designer blouse (one that could cost the price of a suit, if you choose).
- One celebration or special occasion dress.
- One expensive, more distinctive coat.
- One pair of exceptional shoes.
- One luxurious sweater or jacket in soft wool or a wool and silk combination for casualwear.

Stage Five: One-of-a-Kind

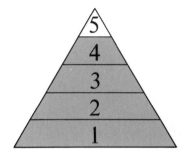

You'll notice that as you've moved from one stage to the next, the number of purchases declined. This is as it should be. You've already invested considerable time, thought, and effort in building the base of a working wardrobe. So now, at Stage Five, you can afford to spend your entire budget on one or two items, if that's what you want. And what you want can be a smashing dress, a coat, or accessories that add to the distinctive personal style you've developed over the years. Now, you can buy the top designers—European, Japanese, or American—who have achieved international fame. You can even purchase a crystal beaded ball gown for this year's gala affair, and wear it once a year or every other year thereafter.

The charts which follow give you the names of suggested designers and manufacturers appropriate for each category. Use them when you plan your shopping.

Category I:
Corporate
Woman

Suits

Traditional matched suits — Tweed, wool crepe, and gabardine

Anne Klein	Ellen Tracy	Ralph Lauren
Anne Klein II	Harvè Bernard	J. G. Hook
Calvin Klein	Dana Buchman	Barry Bricken
Cricketeer	Donna Karan	Jaeger
Stanley Blacker	Austin Reed	Kasper

Blouses

Long-sleeved blouses with simple understated design, often high necked, or accompanied with tie, or softly pleated or shirred with lapel or self-tie.

Levanté	Cricketeer	Dior
Anne Klein II	Omanti	Y. Le ' V
Calvin Klein	Lyle & Scott	Ralph Lauren
Gordon		

Dresses

Finished neck, long-sleeved, belted — Wool, challis, silk — Solid or small consistent print, simple design, often fits under jacket

BUSINESS — Soft, understated

Albert Nipon	Bicci	Harvè Bernard
Calvin Klein	Schraeder	R. Heller
Anne Klein	Cricketeer	PSI
David Hayes	Jerry Sherman	

SOCIAL — Simple, long-sleeved, excellent design, high neck

Albert Nipon	PSI	Dior
R. Warren		

Shoes

Evan Picone	Anne Klein	Ferragamo
Calvin Klein	YSL	David Evins
Valentino		

Suits

Blazer, cardigan, short & other — Close to traditional or traditional sleeves — Mixed jackets and skirts — Sweater as accent or replacement for blouse

Tahari	PSI	Chanel
Perry Ellis	Donna Karan	Prophecy
Dana Buchman	Michael Kors	Bicci
Paul Alexander	Calvin Klein	Liz Claiborne
Ellen Tracy	Claude Montana	Nipon
Sanyo	Kasper	Paul Stanley
Anne Klein II	Anne Klein	

Blouses

More colorful, more design and variety; often main accent of outfit, long sleeve

Argenti	Dior	Ellen Tracy
Anne Klein II	DKNY	Ralph Lauren

Dresses

Similar to Category I without jacket, more colorful but understated, long-sleeved

Liz Claiborne	Ronnie Heller	Steven Stolman
Chetta B	Kenar	St. John Knits
Jerry Regenbogen	St. Gillian	

Business & Social

Understated and simple, more color and design, long-sleeved

Joan Sparks for Daniel Barrett	Raul Blanco	Albert Nipon

Shoes

Anne Klein	Joan & David	Bally
Calvin Klein	Kenneth Cole	Bruno Magli
Amalfi	Pappagallo	

Category II: Communicator Woman

Category III: Creative Woman

Suits
Cardigan or blazer, sleeve accent, jackets—boxy, no lapels, un-constructed, mixed jackets and skirts

Tahari	Carole Little	Sanyo
Anne Klein	Paul Alexander	Donna Karan
Valentino	DKNY	PSI
Calvin Klein	Ellen Tracy	Armani
Perry Ellis		

Blouses
Strong on line and design, many varieties of necklines, sweaters

Tahari	ABS	Anne Klein II
Jerry Regenbogen	Max Studio	

Dresses
Relaxed design, accent on shape and movement, unbelted or drop-waist

BUSINESS & SOCIAL—Dramatic, long, may be short-sleeved

Geoffrey Beene	Bettina Reidel	Carole Little
Ungaro	Yamamoto	Joan Vass

Shoes

Kenneth Cole	Bally	Joan & David
Donna Karan	Bruno Magli	

10

Men: A Suitable Approach

It's no secret that men still have an easier time than their female counterparts in today's business world. In fact, they have a distinct advantage on several fronts. They were there first, already ensconced in the seats of power. And, more germane to this book, they have fewer choices to make when it comes to assembling a wardrobe. With few exceptions, men's styles, over the years, have remained relatively stable—especially in the business world.

After-hours, on the weekend, traveling to the far-reaches, or settling under a palm tree on vacation, men are finding a dizzying array of clothing options in shape, style, pattern, and most of all, in an explosion of colors. A pair of slacks, two sweaters, jeans, sweat shirt, and bath robe simply don't do it anymore! Putting it all together is becoming an art that needs an expert.

If there were times you felt that you did not have the right thing to wear for business, it was probably because your wardrobe was incomplete—there was no *what* to wear! A good wardrobe means that you have something to wear for every occasion, whether you're just starting out or you've been in the business world for ten or more years.

While there is not as much style latitude in men's apparel as there is for women, the same principles I espouse for women apply to men. Your wardrobe is also made up of background pieces, accents,

Man has a quest for structure and order and after a rambling sleep and the uncertainty of facing the unfolding day, he has a yearning for what is known and refined. People, in general, tend to repeat what is safe and certain.
—Dr. Roger B. Granet, *The New York Times*

We all used to joke about a dress that would take a woman 'from the office out to dinner,' but there really is a need for that for men these days. If a man goes out at night, he wants to be dressed up, not uptight.
—Bill Robinson, quoted in *GQ*

pivots, and signatures. What is different is the degree to which you can vary the basic uniform to achieve your own look.

But let's look at what constitutes a really workable wardrobe.

The Compleat Wardrobe

Suits

The background and backbone of any wardrobe is the suit. French designer and perfumer Bernard Lanvin says "A suit is an investment in an atmosphere of living. Businessmen feel better in a solid color. It reflects their experience." (*Bazaar*, April, 1989)

A male wardrobe which goes anywhere consists of eight suits. For most men in Categories I and II, this means traditional American-cut suits: single breasted, two- or sometimes three-buttoned, soft- or natural-shouldered and single vented. A variation on this style is the updated or Ivy League suit—with its slightly built-up shoulder and closer fit at the waist. It is not as fitted as European styles, however. A third style is the double-breasted, peaked lapel suit.

You cannot go wrong in buying a suit, regardless of which Stage you're in or your position at your company, if you choose your suits from a color palette of blue, gray, and tan. The darker the color, the more formal the suit. The lighter the color, the more casual the look. A good blue suit is probably the favorite first choice of most men. In fact, in color tests conducted by psychologists, blue is chosen the favorite over and over again. And within the confines of a blue palette, you will find a range from the darkest navy to the most subtle of muted shades. They are available in solids, pinstripes, chalk stripes, and tick weaves. It is the uniform of Category I businesses.

Gray, a good alternate or perhaps second choice, will take you anywhere. It's not as formal as a really dark blue suit, but it is as assertive. Here, too, you can choose a range from the lightest (but not too light!) to charcoal gray. You could choose very dark gray (often referred to as banker's gray) or charcoal solids in a wool flannel or a lighter weight (such as tropical worsteds) for warmer weather. Another choice might be a dark gray pinstripe or shadow stripe. Other choices include tick weaves, nailheads, subtle herringbones, Donegal tweeds, hard finished worsteds, gray and white glen plaids.

Both blue and gray suits in the standard shades coordinate easily with shirts and ties. These colors, though muted, vary in the jockeying for power.

A good example of the power invested in the dark blue suit occurred in a large Midwestern medical company. The company, in the person of its vice president of Research and Development, developed a product instrumental in the working of transplants. Everything about the product had been tested; it was deemed safe on all fronts. Yet the company could not get the go-ahead from the Food and Drug Administration. The VP of R & D who headed the project and the FDA simply could not come to an agreement. It soon became apparent that their differences had nothing to do with the product; rather, it had more to do with winning a power struggle.

I was brought in to help analyze the situation. I asked the VP to give me a brief description of what each party was wearing. I concluded that the best thing for the VP to do on his next trip to Washington, D.C. was to leave his dark blue suit home. I advised him to wear a medium to light gray suit, and told him that since he had power with the product, he didn't need the personal power the blue suit conferred. What he needed was the OK—in other words, getting what he went for. (P.S.: He got the approval.)

Tan is a variation on the theme of blue and gray and often the choice for summer weight suits. The range of color is not as broad, but it does include khaki, olive, and camel.

Tan is periodically a winter or transitional color accent, especially in a blazer. In less traditional businesses, colors and brands often go "Euro," as in olive, pewter, brown-black, sometimes flecked with threads of deep red, blue, or yellow. Or, a series of dusty, subdued colors can make up the check or stripe pattern in jackets. In summer, the range broadens to include celery, oyster, and a multitude of beautiful colors that blend with neutrals.

Jackets

Jackets or sport coats are a must. Three will give you the versatility you need to go from after-hours to less formal weekend events, from day to evening. They can take you to the office on Fridays, to meet an out-of-town client on a Saturday morning, to a business-related party on Saturday night. They are also a good choice for afternoon events on weekends that involve meeting people. They can

It was the Ivy League look. The style of the silver screen. The suit Frank crooned "All the Way" in. The three-buttoned suit remains traditionally patterned, the suit has a new silhouette for business; easy, fitted, buttoned at the middle for subtle elegance. A far cry from the shapeless, drapeless sack suit of the past, this rethought classic proves good things come in threes.
—GQ

Tweed matches almost everything. And it's never dated.
—Karl Lagerfeld, *Vogue*

also be dressed down with a sweater, and sans tie, to fit into your casualwear wardrobe.

A good navy blazer in a smooth finish should be your first choice, especially if you're just starting out. A second sportcoat might be in camel; and if you choose to purchase it in the later stages of your wardrobing, you might consider a camel's hair or luxurious cashmere. Your third sportcoat might be a subtle wool tweed, or a linen and silk blend tweed in colors that go well with the slacks in your wardrobe.

Slacks

The sportcoats described above should be coordinated with at least four pairs of slacks. For that traditional navy blazer at Stage One, you should buy two pairs of slacks: the first in camel or khaki gabardine, the second in gray flannel. These can be worn with or without the sportcoat, depending on the occasion. Other choices might include herringbones, subtle wool tweeds, and colors which coordinate with the patterned sportcoat.

Shirts

While a navy blue suit and white shirt is never a "wrong" choice, you do have more latitude in choosing shirts. But you risk too much time and money in that suit to undercut it with inappropriate accessories--accessories which send out the wrong message. Shirts offer a wide variety of colors, textures, and moods. Color, pattern, fabric, and style constitute the decisions you make about the shirts in your closet.

Fabric:

All-cotton or a cotton and polyester blend (if it fits with your company culture) are probably the best choices. No matter which you choose, make sure you have the shirts professionally laundered. Home laundered shirts get that "washboard" look because the thread never dries sufficiently. It's worth the extra money to have shirts that are always crisp and professional looking. Nothing looks tackier than a wrinkled collar.

A man's wardrobe needs to be happily balanced. I call it 'strawberries and cream.' I mean basically, you've got the strawberries—things like navy blue suits, chino pants, simple white shirts—then you've got the cream—silly prints.
—Paul Smith, quoted in *GQ*

Style:

The style and cut of your shirt is a strategic decision because the shirt is such an obvious item of clothing. Choose a collar style appropriate to your face and neck. There are straight collars, spread collars, button-downs, or tab collars. The button-down and tab collars are probably the least formal, more at home with a blazer. They are unsuitable for evening wear. Stiffer collars, like the straight and spread, are more formal. Cuffs, too, are important. They come in two varieties: button or barrel (the cuffs found on most shirts), and French cuffs. Every shirt must have a cuff; short sleeves are not an option for business dress.

If the men in your organization wear button-downs, perhaps your industry is, too! Perhaps button-downs indicate not so much the industry as the part of the country your company is located (button-downs are a particular favorite of the Midwest in business and at Ivy League schools). If it is a dress shirt with a white spread collar, there is significance to that choice. Sometimes, these choices fit into the culture, sometimes it's a personal choice. It's important, however, to notice whether or not your personal favorites are part of the culture. If not, it's jarring. How do you know? People will remark, will make jokes or comments. There are many ways to pick up messages about clothes—more often through the gut than the ear.

In Category I and more formal Category II organizations, the traditional full- cut and regular-cut shirts are appropriate choices. Some Category III organizations can tolerate fitted shirts, although it's a matter of location: New York, Chicago, and Atlanta are a few of the cities where you can choose more style in the traditional Categories I and II companies.

Colors:

Standard colors are variations of white and blue. Other choices include Bengal, bold, or fine stripes (the rule of thumb: the narrower the stripe the more conservative the shirt), and tattersall or small checks in gray, blue, red, or khaki or olive. Category III shirts, like suits, include hues from salmon and oyster to lavender and olive.

He took out a pile of shirts and began throwing them, one by one, before us, shirts of sheer linen and thick silk and fine flannel, which lost their folds as they fell and covered the table in many-colored disarray. While we admired, he brought more and the soft rich heap mounted higher—shirts with stripes and scrolls and plaids in coral and apple-green and lavender and faint orange with monograms of Indian blue. Suddenly, with a strained sound, Daisy bent her head into the shirts and began to cry stormily.

'They're such beautiful shirts,' she sobbed, her voice muffled in the thick folds. 'It makes me sad because I've never seen such—such beautiful shirts before.'
—F. Scott Fitzgerald, *The Great Gatsby*

Twelve dress shirts is the minimum you can get away with in your wardrobe. Five white shirts can be chosen from a range of broadcloth, oxford cloth, and pinpoint oxford cloth, from the button-down variety to point collars to spread and tab collars. Three blue and two ecru shirts in the same range should complete the solids in your wardrobe. The last two shirts in this foundation or beginning stage shirt wardrobe can be in pattern. Because the latter will be worn more often, it's probably a good idea to choose subtle, widely spaced stripes rather than the bolder Bengal stripes. As you build a more extensive wardrobe, you can choose shirts with stronger stripes and more widely varied color.

In addition to the twelve dress shirts you need for business, you'll want to add more casual shirts—shirts that can take you out after-hours and lounging around on weekends. A minimum of five casual shirts can give you the versatility to switch your outfits, enabling you to dress up or down.

Outerwear

The substantial investment in coats means that you should buy the best quality you can afford in traditional shapes. The best choices include a wool topcoat in dark blue, dark gray, or black. Choose single-or double-breasted styling with slash or flap pockets. A dressed up, formal look can be found in the Chesterfield, which is a more fitted cut with a slightly suppressed waist and a velvet collar. Because it is a more formal coat which may be inappropriate for daywear, you could add it in the later stages of wardrobing. Tweed coats, which are more casual, can also be chosen at a much later stage.

You'll also need a coat for rainy weather. This coat will take you through many travel situations and climate changes, and because the style varies little from season to season, it can be worn for years. This can be a double-breasted trench coat or a single-breasted variety with a zip-in lining in khaki or tan. These coats come in all price points, from the traditional, top-of-the-line Burberry trench (It really was designed for the military! "When soldiers who had been given these coats returned to the homefront with their 'waterproofs,'" says Ralph DiGennaro, in an article in *Portfolio,* "a new peacetime fashion was forged for civilians.") to lighter weight varieties at half the cost.

In addition to cold weather and rainwear coats, you'll also need one or two casual coats that you can wear on weekends, and at informal events like sports events. Two good choices include the perennial favorite Eisenhower jacket in a good leather or heavy cotton twill and what is typically called a loden or duffel coat. The bomber jacket in leather or khaki twill has been a strong wardrobe piece over the years and it continues to be important, as have a few other "military" fashions—khaki and camouflage shirts and pants, war surplus pants, Navy peacoats.

When buying a business coat, make sure you try it on while wearing a suit. You don't want to be cramped in it. Check your length, too. Coats are being worn longer, so it's important to make sure the length is right for you.

Accessories

Given the narrowly defined looks that are acceptable for most business dress—in suits and shirts—the remaining choices in ties, scarves, braces, shoes, and other items in a good wardrobe provide you with the opportunity to individualize, to accent, so that you can look and feel your best.

Ties

Haberdashers often call a tie a man's "flag" because it serves as a man's single biggest advertisement. The tie is about the only outlet the male exec has to be dashing, says Terry Dobris, vice-president of tie-maker Format, in *Businessweek*. The tie is an area of acceptable eccentricity, says designer Bill Robinson. And while this may be true, because it is a flag, it needs to send out the right signals about your attitude, your taste, and your status. Ties are laden with symbolism (they are representative of what is left of the heraldic shield that accompanied suits of armor). Browse through a large tie department, and you'll notice the lion, the shield, the staff, the Napoleonic fleur-de-lis.

Before reading was widespread, these pictures or signs affixed to shields designated ally or foe enabling armies to know who to attack.

Marlene Dietrich and Bette Davis, two actresses who practically defined the strong-willed woman, were never tougher than when—in *Witness for the Prosecution* and *Deception*, respectively— they were draped in trenches, belts knotted insouciantly and collars turned up a'la Bogie.

But the mystique of the raincoat predates the movies; there is, for instance, the apocryphal story of Lord Kitchener, the great British soldier of the turn of the century, who grew so attached to his government-issue trenchcoat that he elected to be buried in it.
—Ralph DiGennaro, *Portfolio*

Ties really do serve as a foundation. What they enable a man to do is put together different wardrobe looks without buying a different suit for everyday. They offer variation and individuality and jackets are designed in a V-shape, to focus on the tie.

It's a role the tie has played since the 16th century, when King Louis of France admired the

Today, ties are strong identifiers of who's who in the organizational hierarchy by their design, their color, as well as the way they're tied. Too flashy or unusual and you may draw attention away from what you're saying, may cause your audience not to take you seriously.

Never underestimate the importance of your tie. It is one of your first investments. Its quality and costliness is recognized, and often it's the signal that can get you into a good restaurant; sometimes, it will even get you a good table. Forty dollars is not out of line for a good tie, and if you can, choose ties in the fifty to sixty-dollar range.

Ties come in all colors, patterns, and fabrics, but the most suitable for business dress include solids, foulards, repps or stripes, pin-dots, polka dots, and paisleys, predominantly in silk or silk blends. If you're choosing solid ties and you're in a traditional business, I suggest you choose silk and wool challis in such colors as navy, burgundy, and red. Also take note of the color of the current season's power tie. Several years ago, it was red; more recently it was yellow, and today, tiemakers are touting the power of purple (which will lose ground as soon as it becomes obvious). In Category III organizations, ties change color, shapes, and design. Patterns can be wider and wider, and colors run the gamut.

- *Foulards* are silk or silk-blend ties with a small repeat pattern in harmonizing colors. The best background colors for foulards are navy, gray, burgundy, and yellow.

- Striped ties, which are appropriate with nearly every suit and blazer, come in four varieties. The *Repps* are diagonally striped in a ribbed silk. *Regimentals* have a solid background color and two to three narrow bands of color (like the symbols on some ties, these colors did act as regimental identification). Colleges have college ties, and the "cognoscenti" know each other by their ties. *University* stripes are two colors in equally wide bands. Businesses in this country have adopted military and collegiate symbols which now appear as Category I and II business dress. *Blazer* stripes have one dominant band, bisected by a brightly colored stripe alternating with a narrower band of a third color.

- *Paisleys* have an overall, multi-color design in a decorative tear-drop pattern.

Bow ties may be chosen in some business environments, but you have to have a personality that can handle the reactions of your colleagues. And they can be a plus or a minus depending on who you are, the industry you're in, and the Category your organization represents.

Shoes

Shoes should be the best you can afford. They should fit well to provide comfort all day long. Improperly fitted shoes can ruin your day. For starters, you'll need two pairs: one in black and the other in brown or cordovan (mahogany or oxblood) in a lace-up style for Categories I and II. In Category I, black wing tips are probably the most appropriate choice. They go well with either navy or gray suits. For Category III, you can select a slip-on with a low vamp and thin sole. The second pair should also be of the lace-up variety for Categories I and II, perhaps in a cap-toe oxford.

The Duke of Windsor was never one to play it safe, even in matters of personal style. His pattern-mixing panache was legendary, and he caused the second-biggest scandal of his career by wearing brown suede shoes with a gray suit. He might never have ruled Britannia, but he ruled men's style for a generation. . . .
—*GQ*

Hosiery

Only solid, dark, over-the-calf stockings are appropriate in a business environment in Categories I and II. Most men prefer lightweight wool, cotton lisle, and blends of wool and nylon. Black stockings are worn with blue or gray suits. Interesting textures, bolder patterns, and argyles can make up your hosiery selections for casualwear. You should include a minimum of 20 pairs in your wardrobe.

As of this writing, in Category III organizations, patterned socks are a favorite from subtle Euro-designs to bold, outrageous, and irreverent ones. Marshall Sanders, art director for John Ryan & Company, feels socks are too often overlooked. "I have people compliment me on my socks; it makes me feel good because they appreciate my attention to detail. That's what separates me creatively in my work . . . ."

I like socks with different designs on them, different colors. I think sometimes you can make a statement with your socks."
—Danny Glover, quoted in *GQ*

Belts

Belts are a subtle addition to your suit. Don't call attention to your waistline by wearing showy buckles. Your belts should do what they were created for— hold up your pants. Choose two narrow leather

Status watches, whether vintage Audemars Piguet or a 1989 Rolex Oyster, can be effective symbols of power in today's corporate climate. "When you wear a certain kind of watch, you signal how rich and important you are."
— Jack Solomon, quoted in SELF

If the Duke of Windsor were alive today, he'd no doubt tip his Panama hat to the latest additions to a fashionable man's wardrobe: double-breasted suits, brown suede shoes and the latest Duke-inspired fashion rediscovery, the tab-collared shirt. Introduced back in the Thirties, this distinctive dress shirt has a small strip of fabric attached to the collar that fastens underneath a tie by means of either a button, a snap or, most elegant of all, a brass stud (which is how the Duke wore it). Why a tab? 'It's a nice, neat look,' explains Patricia Grodd, merchandising director of New York City's Paul Stuart. 'It holds the tie in place and allows it to belly out rather than lie flat, which gives it a nice hang and a little more dash.' Perhaps the appeal lies in the tab collar's ability to look dressy without being ostentatious.
— GQ

belts, one in black and one in cordovan with understated metal buckles. Both will coordinate with your shoes. While they should be in the same color family, they need not match exactly. Later choices can be patterned leather, lizard or crocodile.

Scarves

Scarves, which come in an unlimited range of pattern and color, add style to any wardrobe. They tuck easily into the collar of your coat, provide warmth, and keep the collar clean. Scarves give your clothes that extra punch, especially if you choose a surprisingly bright color in wool. They can change the overall effect of your outfit as well as your mood. Euro patterns are the best (subtle and expensive Yves St. Laurent, Valentino, Armani, Hugo Boss). Even in a traditional environment, scarves are apropos in a vast selection of design motifs.

You can repeat the color of your coat, for example, or you can choose a surprising contrast. Woolen scarves, in solids or subtle tweeds, are an excellent addition to any wardrobe, as are paisleys or foulards in wool challis.

At later stages in wardrobing, when you feel you can afford to spend a greater percentage of your annual budget on fewer items, you might want to consider a cashmere or silk scarf for that extra dash, that elegant formality. The most formal scarf is a white silk which is worn exclusively for formal or black-tie events.

Pocket Squares

Once you have acquired the basics, you'll want to purchase pocket squares to complement both the color and pattern of your necktie. These come in solids or over-all patterns like paisleys and foulards. You don't want your pocket square to match your tie; rather, it should complement. You might, for instance, be wearing a navy suit, white shirt, and a blue and burgundy repp tie. Then, I suggest you choose a paisley with tones of blue and burgundy dominating.

A silk square peeking out of your pocket adds dash, color, and polish to a suit. There are two ways to wear a pocket square: Fold loosely so that you have four points; then, tuck it into your pocket with the points up or points down, depending on your company's culture (either "they do" or "they don't"), the style of the moment, or the country you're in. Merely be conscious of it, and quickly adapt. Be aware, however, that upper management usually sets the trend.

A man of sense carefully avoids any particular character in his dress; he . . . dresses as well, and in the same manner, as the people of sense and fashion of the place where he is.
—Lord Chesterfield, *Letters to His Son*

The illustrations which follow define the uniforms of Category I, II, and III Business dress.

Category I:
Business

Category II:
Business

Category III:
Business

Casual dress is a different story for men. No uniform here.

Category I:
Casual

Category II:
Casual

Category III:
Casual

Notice the subtle differences in evening dress for each of the Categories.

II

I

III

Evening Wear

Outerwear is an important consideration. The coats illustrated on the following page show three distinct varieties—the traditional double-breasted topcoat for Category I, the raglan-sleeved gabardine for Category II, and the inimitable trench for Category III.

III

I

II

Outerwear

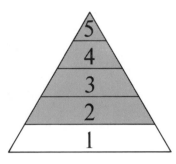

By following the wardrobing guidelines below, you can be well-dressed, regardless of which Category your company belongs in.

Stage One: Starting Out

- Two suits, one in a solid gray or navy. Depending on your first choice, the second in a gray or navy subtle pattern (chalk or windowpane) in a single-breasted, single-vented wool American cut.
- One navy blazer.
- Two pairs of slacks, khaki gabardine and gray flannel.
- One dozen shirts: five white, three blue, two ecru, and two patterned.
- Two pairs of leather shoes, black and cordovan.
- Eight ties: three stripes (repp, university, or blazer); three foulards, and two paisleys. At least two ties should have the background color of the season's power tie.
- Two belts, a black and a cordovan, with simple metal buckles.
- Ten pairs of hosiery in navy, black, and charcoal gray.
- One trench coat, either single- or double-breasted.
- A solid wool top coat in charcoal, navy, black, or camel.
- Black leather attaché case for Categories I and II. Category III men can choose a softer variety, such as an envelope or satchel.
- One pair of casual slacks in a pattern: glen plaid, herringbone, tick weave, or nailshead.
- One pair of navy jeans.
- One cotton or wool crew neck sweater.

Stage Two: Adding Distinction

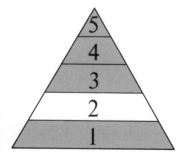

The emphasis in Stage Two can be twofold—acquiring casual and roughwear and expanding your suit collection. Here's what you can add to your base:

- Two more suits, in navy or gray, depending on the choice you made in Stage One. Regardless of which color you select, this can be in a more dominant pattern or a brighter colored pattern. Your second choice should be a brown, tan, or camel, either solid or in a windowpane or glen plaid. With both suits, stick to the traditional or updated American-cut suit.

- One patterned sportcoat in a tweed, herringbone, or plaid that will coordinate with some of the casualwear you chose in Stage One.
- One pair of slacks in a less traditional color, perhaps picking up one of the colors in your patterned sportcoat.
- Six shirts: two replacements for your white shirts and four in solids and patterns. Here, you might experiment with pale pink or yellow in the solids, or bold stripes in red or navy.
- Four ties: two silk paisleys and two linen or knit ties in colors which complement your sportcoat and navy blazer.
- One additional belt in either black or dark brown.
- One pair of braces in a complementary rather than matching color.
- One pair of navy or gray brushed-cotton slacks.
- Three cotton or wool sweaters. For a more casual look, one choice can be a shawl-collared wool cardigan which can be worn in place of a jacket for a more casual look. Two V-neck or crew neck pullovers, one a solid, the other in a pattern. Here, you can experiment with color and pattern—lavenders, teals, and pinks.
- One casual outerwear jacket. At this stage, the most appropriate and cost-conscious variety would be a heavy cotton twill, either the Eisenhower jacket or duffel coat, in a color that complements your basic casual and roughwear.
- One pair of black jeans.
- Two or three heavier cotton shirts.
- One pair of heavier soled shoes or boots.
- One pair of athletic footwear.

Stage Three: Panache

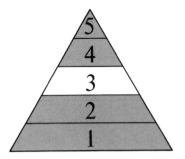

Now that you've spent your budget on acquiring the basics, you can add a little flair to your wardrobe. You can be more daring with color. You can look for signatures and accents that enhance to your personal style.

- Two suits, one in a double-breasted Euro-style (some of the outstanding collections are by Armani, Hugo Boss, Pierre Cardin, Bill Robinson, Bill Kaisermann, and Valentino). The second suit should be a solid black or tuxedo for formal wear.

- One "black tie" or tuxedo shirt with a pleated front and point collar. This should be in white only. Even though formalwear shops advertise ruffles and color, these are not appropriate.
- Four dress shirts, perhaps with tab collars and French cuffs.
- One pair of dress shoes in black patent leather or a patent and suede combination.
- Two vests in tapestry or knit to wear for a dressy casual event.
- Two Euro-style slacks.
- Four pocket silks in complementary colors.
- One pair of classic cuff links, at this stage, if you select French cuffed shirts.
- One set of cuff links and studs for formalwear.

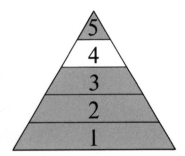

Stage Four: Self indulgence

You will notice as you move from stage to stage you are buying fewer and fewer pieces. When you get to this stage, you should probably spend a considerable percentage of your annual budget on a few really expensive pieces. Now, you can afford to choose such upscale items as:

- An Oxxford suit made to measure.
- Three absolutely exquisite shirts, custom-tailored in the finest cotton.
- Two pairs of Italian or French shoes.
- A luxurious terry cloth robe for lounging.
- A wonderful silk scarf.
- Italian leather gloves.
- Leather casual jacket.

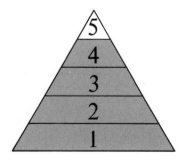

Stage Five: One-of-a-Kind

You have been careful with your budget. You have shopped for the best. Don't stop now. A wonderful choice for more formal dressing might be a cashmere polo coat or a tuxedo coat. This is also the time to invest in a gold watch. And if you like the special treatment you get with custom tailoring, you might wish to add a custom-made suit in a lightweight woolen.

The charts on the following pages suggest of designers and manufacturers appropriate for each of the Categories. Use them when you plan to shop.

Category I:
Corporate Man

Suits
Traditional style and colors

Hart Schaffner & Marx	Cricketeer	Hickey Freeman
Austin Reed	Norman Hilton	Bill Blass
Brooks Brothers	Oxxford	Christian Dior
Chaps	Polo Ralph Lauren	Polo University
Calvin Klein	Lanvin	

Sport Coats
Traditional style and color

Hart Schaffner & Marx	Cricketeer	Palm Beach
Austin Reed	Stanley Blacker	Christian Dior
Calvin Klein	Polo University	Bill Blass

Shirts
Basic colors/blue, white, ecru

Oxford	Damon	Arrow
Hathaway	Geoffrey Beene	Henry Grethel
Polo	Eagle	Grant

Shoes

Cole Hahn	Bally	Nunn Bush
Johnston Murphy	Weejun	Freeman

Ties
Rep, club, and foulard

Hathaway	Northbriar	Polo
Countess Mara	Pulitzer	Briar

Category II: Communicator Man

Suits
Somewhat traditional, more color and texture

Austin Reed	Cricketeer	Christian Dior
Evan Picone	Bill Blass	Geoffrey Beene
Calvin Klein	Chaps	

Sport Coats
Somewhat traditional, more color and texture

Austin Reed	Cricketeer	Hart Schnaffer & Marx
Polo Ralph Lauren	Christian Dior	Bill Blass
Calvin Klein		

Shirts
White, all pastels, pin stripes and fancies

Gant	Calvin Klein	Arrow
Hathaway	Christian Dior	John Henry
Geoffrey Beene		

Shoes

Cole Hahn	Bally	Nunn Bush
Bill Blass	Weejun	Freeman

Ties
Stripes and foulard

Christian Dior	Bill Blass	Pulitzer
Calvin Klein		

Suits
Fashion forward in design, color, and texture

Giorgio Armani	Bill Blass	Perry Ellis
Pierre Cardin	Daniel Hechter	Henry Grethel
YSL	Hugo Boss	Bill Robinson
Nino Cerruti	Claude Montana	Andrew Fezza
Calvin Klein	Valentino	Ronaldus Shamask

Sport Coats
Fashion forward in design, color and texture

Giorgio Armani	Daniel Hechter	Hugo Boss
Pierre Cardin	Calvin Klein	Claude Montana
YSL	Bill Blass	Perry Ellis
Nino Cerruti	Jones NY	

Shirts
All colors and hues, bold stripes and patterns, fancies

John Henry	Geoffrey Beene	Armani
Daniel Hechter	Arrow Brigade	Perry Ellis
Calvin Klein	Byblos	Kenneth Cole
Christian Dior	Andrew Fezza	Liz Claiborne

Shoes

Cole Hahn	Bill Blass	Amalfi
Bally	Mascolini	Ferragamo

Ties
Stripes, foulard and paisley

L'Homme	Calvin Klein	Perry Ellis
Armani	Bill Blass	Hugo Boss
Bill Robinson	Valentino	

*Category III:
Creative Man*

11

The Shopping Solution

What do people most dislike about shopping? Crowds, the bewildering sea of merchandise, harried and indifferent salespeople, lines at the fitting room and cash registers, and most frustrating of all, not finding anything that's right after the ordeal.
— *Working Woman*

Shopping takes thought, time, effort, and energy. For some, it means taking a deep breath and getting on with it. For others who absolutely hate it, it means getting it done, getting it over with. But whatever your attitude, it's not something you can put off indefinitely, especially when your present and future depend on how you present yourself to the world.

When you decide to invest your money in financial ventures, it often becomes a fascinating game: You pour over books, magazines, and newspapers hoping to find a format for "investing smart," a map to financial independence. If you haven't time to do that, you consult with a financial planner, with your accountant, your broker — experts who know the ropes, the system, the territory.

If you believe, as I do, that clothing is an investment, then the same thought, effort, and energy that goes into planning is also required in pulling together a wardrobe that works, a wardrobe that pays a return. Some of us have no choice. We have to shop for ourselves. We can't, very often, delegate the task to someone else.

Shopping is an inevitability — almost as much as "death and taxes." Yet men and women alike sometimes feel insecure at the thought of shopping for clothes. This insecurity stems from the discomfort in having to make choices, as well as the apprehension of spending money to make an appropriate presentation, and even the uncertainty about the image one wants to project.

For some, it's an unpleasant experience because they find it over-whelming, and confusing; there's too much of a sensory assault and too many choices. This is especially true of men who are not used to multi-level dressing. They are not comfortable with the premium put on dressing appropriately for life style, occasion, and event.

Shopping requires making a decision about the way you present yourself to the world. Because all cultures breed conditioned responses and reactions, be aware and in control of how you look. Choosing among all the items available and parting with hard-earned money is an investment decision of some consequence. Throughout this book, I keep stressing the fact that dress and presentation are vi-tal because they are the keys to appearing and feeling confident and being credible.

Our usual, almost flippant, approach to shopping — on the run, during lunch hours, and at odd unexpected moments — is not the way to make this kind of investment. Yet we find it hard to take the time to scout the stores in our city, to pour over fashion magazines, and to actually set aside time to shop. Since our time is so limited, our lives more pressured, it's even more important to shop with a plan. And that's what this section of the book is all about — shopping with a plan. Mortimer Levitt, founder of The Custom Shop, in his book *Class*, says, "Chief executives know they cannot run a business without a plan. . . . In the same way it is not possible to make efficient use of your clothing budget [and shopping time] without a plan."

You've already started working on your plan: you've cleaned out your closets, you've filled out the Inventory at the end of this book, and you know what you need to shop for — regardless of which Stage you're in.

To give you an additional leg up in shopping your plan, we've in-cluded guidelines for each Category of business dressing, male and female alike. These guidelines, which can be found at the end of chapters nine and ten, include the designers and manufacturers that work best in each category. In addition, it's also important to shop with some fundamentals in mind as explained below.

I hate buying new clothes. I am not scared by the sight of blood, but the clerks in men's cloth-ing shops so terrify me with their traditional cheery greeting of 'Can I help you, sir?' — which, translated freely, means, 'You obviously can't afford anything on sale here, you bum' — that I only dare confront them when bolstered by sufficient drink.

Even then, or possibly as a consequence, I will buy anything rather than be dismissed as an eco-nomic underachiever. Shoes that pinch. Shirts that choke. Tweed trou-sers that itch worse than poison ivy and sport jackets either a size too large or too small. My clothes closet, such as it is, is filled with outra-geously expensive items that I wouldn't be caught wearing in public.
— Mordecai Richler, "Would you buy a used schmutter from this man?"
— GQ

Multi-use: How many combinations can I make?

Regardless of your annual clothing budget, it's important that you look for multi-functional clothes. This is especially true if you're just beginning your career or starting at Stage One. You want a minimal number of pieces to go just about anywhere—from the most formal events to the most casual. You can do this if you shop for classic, simple styles that can be dressed up or down simply by changing accessories, shirt color, or adding sweaters. Early in Stage One of the Pyramid, you want to stay away from trendy clothes in unusual colors. If this is a season where acid green is "in," for example, you should probably think twice about investing in what is sure to have a limited season or limited appeal. But if you really want to buy something in acid green, choose something in an accent grouping—a scarf, a pocketsquare, a headband. You'll feel up-to-date with a touch of the color, and you won't have invested too much in something that could have limited wearability.

Along with having clothes which function in a multitude of settings, you want to have clothes which are multi-use; that is, they work with other clothes in your closet. You want to have shirts that go with all your jackets, blouses that expand the versatility of your suits. You'll want slacks that complement your jackets. Always ask yourself when buying a garment: Where am I going to wear this? If it can go to dinner parties, to conventions, to formal business meetings, and on the road, you know that you're looking at a multi-use item. Furthermore, you want to see if it works with the other pieces you have in your closet. If it only goes with one or two items, perhaps you had better reconsider this investment until a later Stage. This is especially important in Stage One, where you can't afford to buy items that have limited use.

The key is to have fewer clothes that work with everything and take you everywhere. You want to double the visual value of your wardrobe. Let expensive silk ties and scarves and excellent leather gloves carry the day.

Quality: Spend 2x as much on 1/2 as many

Since you'll be buying fewer clothes by following the wardrobing techniques outlined in this book, you'll want to invest in the best quality you can afford. Remember, you want to get out of the trap of having a closet full of clothes with nothing to wear. If you consistently choose quality, you'll never tire of your wardrobe; it will take you from season to season and will last a long, long time.

A good rule of thumb when you're considering the quality of an item: Spend twice as much and buy half as much. Become acclimated to the idea of spending more than you have in the past, but don't sacrifice quality for style.

Shop Your Plan; Stick to Your Budget

Everything I've been talking about so far means that you'll have to shop a plan. You'll have your inventory which tells you what you need at which stage. You'll know what you already have on hand and in what colors, textures, and styles. Don't deviate from the plan. If you consistently follow it, you're less likely to make mistakes by last minute frantic binge shopping, impulse buying, or shopping when you're depressed.

It's a good idea to plan on shopping at least two or three times a season, buying a number of items each time. Shopping item by item or piece by piece, you're sure to make mistakes. Here's an example. You see an absolutely divine blouse or a particularly handsome jacket. On impulse, you snap it up, only to find when you get it home that the color is slightly off or the lapels the wrong shape to balance the other pieces in your wardrobe.

But when you shop and buy several pieces at a time, you can easily see how they work together and how they do or don't complement one another. Also by trying on the pieces together, you can discover a number of ways to change and increase their use and effectiveness.

Again, let me emphasize how important it is that you stay within your budget, unless, of course, the clothing or accessory under consideration is a background or signature piece. You must *resist* the impulse to buy when you've already depleted your year's allocation. You know how much you can invest, and I've shown you how you can get what you need whether your budget is $800, $1,500, or $2,500 annually.

Ones, Only Ones, Please!

By now, you probably have a pretty good idea what you do and don't like, what's appropriate for who you are, what you do, and the way you live. You've spent a good deal of time cleaning out your closet, and you're confident about your "ones." When you shop, then, ask yourself whether you've chosen a "one." You'll know intuitively and immediately. It will feel good, it will look good, and it will work with the rest of your wardrobe.

Remember the time you passed up a perfectly wonderful item? That was a "one"—and today, perhaps five years later, you still remember the "one" you passed up. If it's a good choice, even if it's more than you're used to paying, it will be well worth the extra money as time goes by. Substituting a "two" for a more expensive "one" —putting clothes in your closet that don't get worn very often, that don't work—will put you back where you started when you began this book. If you have any hesitation about an item, it's probably a "two," and no matter how hard you try, you won't ever like it, and it will never work for you.

Know Your Stores

Just as you consult consumer guides for appliances, boats, and cars, you've got to research the stores in your city and the departments within those stores. Once you're familiar with the offerings, you'll be able to eliminate some of the anxiety that shopping creates. You'll even know whether you're in a Category I, II, or III department. It's a great way to edit the options. You'll be able to shop with the knowledge that you can find what you need to complement your wardrobe. You won't have to search endlessly and end up frustrated about having spent time with nothing to take home.

It's also a good idea to find a salesperson you can trust, one you can depend on because when you have established a good customer-salesperson relationship, the latter often keeps track of what you have in your wardrobe and what works for you. It's important to share your shopping plan with this person. Then, he or she can put together items that will work for you in the proper sizes and colors. A knowledgeable, efficient salesperson will cut down on *your* shopping time.

So find your source, let him or her know you want to become a client, and you'll find you have an expert who can take over and carry out what might be, for you, a miserable task. One of the real benefits of this strategy is that you'll get a very centered style because you'll be developing it with one person, not five or six, each of whom are competent, but naturally quite different.

Work a Personal Shopping Service

Retail businesses today are undergoing massive changes, as are many other industries. As a result, you will find many businesses concentrating more and more on a combination of service and expertise.

Many large retail chains have personal shopping services. Check them out. At Dayton's in Minnesota and Hudson's in Michigan, FYI Personal Shopping and Wardrobing Service is an extraordinarily good service. I know because I founded it 12 years ago, have constantly refined the method, and trained an expert staff. These consultants with their extensive training know how to easily work with you to meet your shopping and wardrobing needs. They know what you have in your closet. They know you—your personality, your lifestyle, your personal style, and your budget. In effect, they know your likes, dislikes, and your monetary constraints. Because they do, they can edit the store for you. They can assemble everything you need in one location with a minimum of time and fuss. One of my FYI clients said: "It's like going home to mother's where she does everything for you."

A good shopping service takes the anxiety and frustration out of shopping and lets you shop for more in less time. The gratifying result is that you end up with a higher quality wardrobe within your budget—a wardrobe which can power you to greater career heights.

Appendix

The Inventory for Women and Men on the following pages can be used after you've cleaned your closets.

1. List the clothes you have remaining in your closet by type in the column labeled Existing Wardrobe.

2. Then, consult either Chapter 9 (for women) or Chapter 10 (for men) for the additional items you'll need to complete your wardrobe. Remember: What you need depends on the Stage you're in.

3. Refer to the charts which list manufactures and designers suitable for your category in Chapter 9 or 10.

4. Take the Inventory shopping with you, or share it with your personal shopper.

INVENTORY: WOMEN

	EXISTING WARDROBE	
	DESCRIPTION	COLOR
Jackets		
Skirts		
Blouses/Sweaters		
Dresses		
Outerwear		
Shoes		
Accessories		
After-hours and Weekend Dressing		

INVENTORY: WOMEN

	WARDROBE NEEDS	
	DESCRIPTION	COLOR
Jackets		
Skirts		
Blouses/Sweaters		
Dresses		
Outerwear		
Shoes		
Accessories		
After-hours and Weekend Dressing		

INVENTORY: MEN

	EXISTING WARDROBE	
	DESCRIPTION	COLOR
Suits		
Sport Coats		
Slacks		
Shirts		
Ties		
Shoes		
Outerwear		

INVENTORY: MEN

	WARDROBE NEEDS	
	DESCRIPTION	COLOR
Suits		
Sport Coats		
Slacks		
Shirts		
Ties		
Shoes		
Outerwear		